THE
Savvy
FLIGHT INSTRUCTOR

Secrets of the Successful CFI

THE
Savvy
FLIGHT INSTRUCTOR

Secrets of the Successful CFI

BY
GREGORY N. BROWN

FOREWORD BY SEAN E. ELLIOTT
Executive Director of the National Association of Flight Instructors

A FOCUS SERIES BOOK
Aviation Supplies & Academics, Inc.
Newcastle, Washington

The Savvy Flight Instructor
by Gregory N. Brown

Aviation Supplies & Academics, Inc.
7005 132nd Place SE
Newcastle, Washington 98059-3153

Published 1997 by Aviation Supplies & Academics, Inc.

Printed in the United States of America

06   05   04   03   9   8   7   6   5   4   3

ISBN 1-56027-296-1
ASA-SFI

Library of Congress Cataloging-in-Publication Data:

Brown, Gregory N., 1953–
    The savvy flight instructor: secrets of the successful CFI /
    by Gregory N. Brown.
        p.   cm.
    "ASA's Focus series"—Series t.p.
    ISBN 1-56027-296-1
    1. Flight training.   I. Title.
    TL710.B72   1997
    629.132′52′071—DC21   97-29694
                                                 CIP

Cover snapshots: savvy flight instructor Dorothy Schick of TakeWING, Inc.,
congratulates KidFLIGHT™ participants David and Chris Bellitt, their mother
JoAnn Coker; and new pilot Jason Tand.

Brochures on pp. 78, 79, and 205 courtesy TakeWING, Inc.

Historical aviation illustrations © 1996 Zedcor, Inc. All rights reserved, worldwide.
Used with permission.

The engine is the heart of an aeroplane,
but the pilot is its soul.

Sir Walter Raleigh
War in the Air, 1922

CONTENTS

F O U R : *Converting Prospects into Flight Students*   43

T H I R T E E N : *Business and Professional Opportunities: Your Future as an Instructor* **199**

F O U R T E E N : *Legacy of an Instructor: the Privilege and the Glory* **209**

FOREWORD

by Sean E. Elliott

Executive Director of the National Association of Flight Instructors

Congratulations! You are a flight instructor. The congratulations is both deserved and recognized. Whether you are a brand-new instructor or a thirty-year veteran, you play the most critical role in today's aviation industry. Whether you teach part-time, full-time, at a large flight school, or at a small flying club, you share the most innate and important responsibilities in general aviation.

Flight instructing is not overly complicated or difficult. It is, however, unforgiving of the insincere and the ill-prepared. It is an onus upon us as educators to seek new ways of delivering our message. Only those who invest enthusiasm and effort through innovation will reach each flight student as an individual.

Greg Brown's book will open your eyes with thought-provoking insights and techniques that will foster your effectiveness with students. It is an educator's tool that you will consult over and over again. Unlike any other flight instructor resource, *The Savvy Flight Instructor* focuses on elements of teaching and instructor/student relationships that are all but missing in past fundamental textbooks.

It is easy to lose sight of our students' basic needs during the day-to-day rigors of flight training. Greg not only makes you think about how the instructor and student view each other during training situations, he also provides helpful methods to increase your ability to relate as a professional. Here is a "real-world" approach that makes this book a tremendous asset to the aviation educator.

Communication skills are critical to the ultimate success of a quality instructor. As accomplished pilots, we have spent countless hours honing our tactile skills and developing hand-eye coordination through mastery of the flying machine. How much of our efforts have gone toward improving our ability to transfer thoughts, ideas, and concepts to another human being? Mastery of instruction hinges upon the ability to communicate effectively and appropriately, and *The Savvy Flight Instructor* addresses communication like no other book I've read. Communicating is intertwined with every element of its message. From new students to repeat business, Greg shows you different ways to connect with each student and keep them coming back. This kind of advice is priceless! It is what every instructor should learn from day number one.

Another key element to successful instructing is marketing. Greg gives the reader practical ideas and suggestions on how to best reach out to potential students, and valuable tips on keeping students' interest once they are in the door. Most importantly, you do not have to hold a degree in business management to understand and employ these techniques. Your overall outreach and retention will greatly benefit from reading this book.

What about motivation? Surely all successes in mentoring revolve around being a true inspiration to your students. You have reached them, you've kept them coming back, now all that is left is to inspire them to rise higher and higher through dedication and devotion. *The Savvy Flight Instructor* recommends to you philosophical and practical mindsets that will foster a love for flying in all your students.

As a flight instructor, you are, above all else, the instiller of safety and the quality control for our entire industry. *The Savvy Flight Instructor* will show you new ways of evaluating judgment and remind you of old pitfalls that can be dangerous if not kept in check. Put it all together and you have a guide and source of information that will truly affect you and your students.

This book is for the instructor who is out there making it happen. It may not fulfill the needs of those looking for a higher level of technical jargon and a new source of complex diagrams. Rather, *The Savvy Flight Instructor* touches on concepts and ideas that hit home, where the rubber meets the road — that is, in you, the flight instructor. The only test this book will prepare you for is the one of life.

If you want to learn what can really help you as a professional educator in aviation, this is the book for you.

Sean E. Elliott

PREFACE

by the author

The regulations and the *Aeronautical Information Manual* rest battle-worn on your shelf, and you've finally wrapped up one of the toughest orals of your flying career. You're sharp on the fundamentals of instruction, and can identify every one of those different student personality types. You can now fly and talk at the same time, all from the right seat. You can write lesson plans in your sleep, enter mysterious endorsements in student logbooks, and actually explain the finer points of a lazy eight. That's everything you'll ever need to know in order to flight instruct … no more questions, right? Just get on with the instructing, and finally you can get paid to fly.

Yeah, right! Like being all dressed up with no place to go, as the saying goes. This book is designed to help out with all of those "other" flight instructing questions, like where do flight students come from? And once you've got them, how do you keep them flying? How can you optimize your pass rate on checkrides? And how do you get students to come back to you for their advanced ratings?

Along with tips on how to attract and retain flight students, we're going to examine professionalism in flight instructing. In short, how to use your instructing activities to advance your personal flying career, while increasing student satisfaction and promoting general aviation at the same time.

ACKNOWLEDGEMENTS

I am grateful to many people for their help and inspiration during development of *The Savvy Flight Instructor*. Ours is a diverse and complex activity, and there are as many good approaches to its practice as there are instructors, so one never stops learning.

First, a special thanks to those kind enough to review drafts of my manuscript and provide suggestions for enhancements. Warren Smith and J.C. Boylls shared their professional expertise as training managers and pilot examiners. Joe Geare represented CFIs-in-training, while Karen York provided the student pilot perspective on flight training. Steve Lofgren and Melissa Murphy shared their aviation business expertise, and Sean Elliott of NAFI was gracious enough to pen the foreword for this book.

Others who contributed inspiration, anecdotes, advice and moral support impacting this book include Dorothy Schick, Jim Hackman, Ed Helmick, Dick Collins, Tom Payne, Mark Holt, David Holt, Mike Macey, Tom Rishar, Uwe Goehl, David Goodman, Mike Mullis, Gary Worden, Linda Winters, and Barbara Barrett, to name just a few.

My appreciation goes out to the many fine people who through their professionalism have directly or indirectly influenced my philosophy and performance as a flight instructor. Among them are Tom Carney, Shane LoSasso, Terry Harshbarger, Margaret Statzell, Mitch Grundman, Rory Higman, Greg Roberts, Alan Altman, Bob Vetter, Doug Rossman, and MaryEllen Clinkingbeard.

Finally, a special word to the many other instructors and flight students who have taught and inspired me over the years, through both good example and bad. I deeply hope to have contributed at least a small fraction to your success in aviation, especially when compared with all I've gained in return. Thanks to every one of you!

Greg Brown

ONE

A Very Special Club

Have you ever thought about your good fortune to be a flight instructor? Consider the great thrills of your life. For most of us, those first flying lessons rank high on the list. None of us forgets the flight instructors who gave us the foundation of a truly unique career.

As instructors, each of us owns the special opportunity, and earns the special thrill that comes from introducing our students to the joys of flying. Sure, instructing has its problems. It's a lot of work; the pay is rarely anything to brag about, and we're not always as well recognized in the industry as perhaps we should be.

Yet I challenge you to find many pilots who've ever instructed and now regret the experience. Instructing is truly at the heart of aviation. From the grassroots of new student starts all the way up to pilot competency checks on a Boeing 777, instructors are the spark plugs (igniters, for you turbine pilots) that make aviation "go."

MORE THAN JUST PASSING THROUGH…

If you're like many pilots, you regard instructing as a necessary way station along your road to a flying career. Just passing through, you might say. But if you're going to earn the respect it takes to attract students to invest their hard-earned money with you, your instructing career has to be more than just passing through.

What you teach tomorrow in a Cessna, a Warrior, or a Katana may very well impact the safety of tens of thousands of passengers over the lifetimes of your students. Next time you meet someone who's been flying for many years, ask about that pilot's long-ago instructors. Then ask about the occasions when the faces and words of those past teachers have reappeared to help that pilot at critical moments.

It was my fourth or fifth lesson, some twenty-five years ago. My instructor Bob, and I were practicing stalls. "Keep the ball in the middle," Bob urged me repeatedly. Somehow the strength of a young college kid just didn't seem enough to center that little circle at the bottom of the turn coordinator.

Suddenly the horizon started flopping…seemed like the nose of our little Cessna 150 swung straight into a spinning Earth. After the first long moments of panic I looked over at Bob. I can see him clearly to this day in the right seat, relaxed, his arms crossed as we spun out of control.

"Bobbbbb!" I yelled.

Bob slowly turned his head and looked at me. "Well, what're you gonna do about it?" he asked, with an air of total calm.

"I don't knoooooww!!!"

"We're in a spin, right?" came the measured reply. "How do you get out of a spin?" Not the hint of a wrinkle disturbed his brow.

I was too scared to think or answer.

"Opposite rudder, and nose down," Bob told me. In fact I think he told me that three or four times. Bob never did touch the controls, nor even uncross his arms. I made the recovery myself, armed with his advice. It was one of my earliest lessons, but since that day I've never doubted my ability to identify and escape a spin.

I haven't spoken with Bob in years. He left the FBO just after I finished my Private Pilot Certificate, reportedly to enter the seminary. (I've always hoped that flying with me wasn't the only reason he "got religion.")

I now know that my first experience with spins probably wasn't much different than yours or anyone else's. I seriously doubt that Bob would remember me if I ran into him tomorrow. Yet, he looms large in my memory. I learned some important things from him about both flying and instructing which remain with me in a big way today. I suspect that you feel the same way about your first instructor.

Other instructors later taught me their own tricks and secrets of flying. Their faces, too, appear to me at appropriate times: instrument and multi-engine flying, descent planning in jets; motivating students, dealing with weather, contending with emergencies.

Now put yourself in that instructor's seat. As a CFI you own the greatest independence, and in some respects the greatest responsibility you will experience in your flying career. Your opportunities to promote aviation and impact flight safety are tremendous.

The details of the specific lesson you give tomorrow will not likely stay with you for long. Your full schedule over the next few weeks will probably erase it. But your student will remember what happens at tomorrow's lesson in great detail. If you do a good job, you'll set the tone for at least one other pilot's safe and smart operations for many years to come. That's professionalism — whether you instruct only for the next six months, or for the next forty years.

As a flight instructor, I want to be remembered for the right reasons after tomorrow's lesson, and I'll bet you feel the same way. In one sense, we're the ones who make airplanes fly. In every sense, we're the ones who make pilots fly. Welcome to a very special club.

Positive Rate of Climb: Getting Your Career Off the Ground

It's all too easy to pigeonhole the role of flight instructor in the world of aviation. "A step-up job," or "paying your dues"; we hear these kinds of derogatory remarks much of the time. The fact is, at least in the United States, the flight instructor is the single most influential individual in ensuring the long-term availability of civilian pilots, and therefore the health of civil aviation as we know it today.

Along with our primary mission of training pilots, CFIs operate at the grass-roots level of aviation, attracting people to join the aviator ranks, and instilling in them the confidence and enthusiasm to continue flying, be it for pleasure or as a career.

This long-term view is important for the future of our own livelihoods in aviation—not only do new pilots finance flight training, but those who remain active invest in additional certificates and ratings. They rent aircraft, patronize aviation books and magazines, support manufacturers and retailers of aviation supplies and equipment, and ultimately buy airplanes. Think of it: What would general aviation be like without those thousands of flight instructors who attract new blood into the pilot ranks every day?

Promoting aviation means attracting others to invest their hard-earned time and money in learning to fly. In a broader sense, there's also the need to "sell" general aviation to others in the public who may themselves never learn to fly. Accordingly, each of us must take every opportunity to spread the good word about airplanes, how airports contribute to a community, how flying impacts the economy, and how the vast majority of pilots go to great lengths to be good neighbors.

Our mission in the next few chapters will be to examine how you, as an individual flight training professional, can be most effective in recruiting, training, and retaining flight students.

THE CFI'S ROLE IN RECRUITING NEW STUDENTS

Few pilots set out to be independent freelance flight instructors — that is, to line up their own students and be their own bosses. Rather, most new CFIs begin instructing to gain their first aviation employment: to get hired by a flight school where it's finally possible to build flight experience and get paid for it, rather than personally funding every hour in the airplane.

"Why, then, do I have to line up my own students?" one might legitimately ask, "I just need to get a job; my employer will provide the students."

This concern is certainly reasonable, and there are indeed CFIs who have never personally had to beat the bushes to bring in their own students. But at the same time, recruiting students comes with the territory in many CFI positions. And your success as an instructor, both professionally and financially, is almost always influenced by every new student you recruit on your own.

Below are just a few of the many good reasons for honing your student recruiting skills. In later chapters, we'll cover how to do this.

Recruiting Students Will Help You Land a CFI Job

Not yet employed as a CFI? Then by now you've undoubtedly talked to some of your friends who instruct, and perhaps called on a few FBOs (fixed-base operators) and flight schools about positions. However busy a given flight school may be, there's rarely a shortage of instructors. Not enough flight students, perhaps, but plenty of instructors.

Your friends have probably told you some other interesting things about the difficulties of cinching your first instructing job, like how flight schools give preference to their own graduates, but rarely have enough business to hire them all. If the flight school where you trained won't take you, you're caught in the "Catch 22" of not being a graduate of the others! No wonder new CFIs often find themselves in the tough spot of being unemployed with no students, with a few training debts as part of the bargain. Instructing jobs are not always easy to come by.

So what's the secret for getting hired into that entry-level CFI job? It's simple: bring in your own students!

Flight schools are in business to train pilots, so without students they're lost. And the only reason a flight school wouldn't be hiring CFIs would be—not enough students. Sure, customers who walk in the front door of a flight school on their own initiative will be assigned to the "regular instructors." But any students you bring in on your own are "gravy"—additional business that the school might not have recruited without your help.

Think of it: You walk in the door of your first-choice flight school employer, and begin with the following proposition.

"Hi, my name is John Flysgood; I'm a CFI with three primary students lined up, and I'm looking for a place to instruct. Can you help me out?" No manager in his or her right mind is going to turn down new business without a darned good reason.

That flight school will want you not only because you've brought along new business, but also because customer recruiting skills are harder to find than piloting skills. A big part of an instructor's job at any FBO is to attract business. If you can help recruit students, along with doing a professional job of instructing, you'll be an invaluable asset to the operator even with limited flight experience.

Recruiting Students Will Make You Busy — Sooner

Even instructors lucky enough to find positions often end up doing a lot less flying than they'd like. The reason for this is the tough-to-crack flight school tradition of full-time versus part-time employees.

The way it works is that most flight schools employ one or more "full-time instructors" who are paid a salary or flight-hour minimum, plus flight pay and perhaps some employment benefits. Full-timers are necessary at flight schools so the manager can be sure someone will be around all the time to take care of walk-ins and other unscheduled business.

"Part-time" or "freelance" instructors, on the other hand, are paid only per hour of instruction given, even though they may hang around the flight school sixty hours per week. Since the full-timers are already being paid just to be there, it's no surprise that the FBO steers most or all new walk-in customers to them. The objective is to occupy the salaried full-timers first, then use part-timers to fill in when extra capacity is needed. Since most new instructors are usually hired on part-time status, that first CFI job can turn out to be a bit of a surprise.

"We'll take you on," says the flight school manager, "but all of our current students are called for. Any students you pick up on your own are yours to keep." In short, you're hired but you need to find your own students. Even having lined up a job, new instructors often must fend for themselves in order to do any flying.

The Right Flight Students Will Advance Your Career

One might think, "once I get established as a regular instructor, I won't need to do any recruiting." This is not necessarily true. In any business there are slow periods when instructors can benefit by getting out there and beating the bushes for new students. Not only does a continuing supply of flight students help pay the bills, but those slow periods don't do anything to build flight experience for pilots desiring an airline job down the road.

Speaking of careers, what about instrument time? Hours in high-performance aircraft? And that multi-engine experience everyone craves? Even busy CFIs are faced with recruiting challenges, such as attracting advanced and multi-engine students in order to move up into bigger airplanes.

Another good reason to hone your recruiting skills is that attracting the right flight students can lead to exciting career opportunities. Professional people, for example, make terrific flight students because they can afford to fly as much as they want, and then often go on to buy airplanes. Plus, they tend to have plenty of contacts.

If a successful business owner signs up to take lessons from you and enjoys the experience, what will she end up flying in a year or two? Hard to predict, but she may need someone to fly her King Air when she's too busy to do it herself. Then when you're ready to proceed to the next step in your own career, there's a good chance that business owner has some friends or business associates who can help you out. (Providing you've done a great job for her, that is.)

I can assure you that these sorts of lucky breaks do occur, because it happened to me. My first multi-engine pilot job came about when a newly instrument-rated student of mine telephoned. "This flying yourself around is great stuff!" he said. "I've decided to buy a multi-engine airplane for my company. Want to come fly it for us?"

Recruiting such people into flying usually pays off for everybody. My student was pleased to have discovered an enjoyable new way to improve travel efficiency in his company. The flight school manager was happy because the student bought the plane from his FBO, hangared it there, and had all his maintenance performed on site. And there's no need to tell you how I felt about the plan. In short, having top-quality students is a good deal for everyone.

With More Students You Can Be Selective

Another reason for recruiting your own students may be less obvious. If you've been instructing for long, or have talked with your own instructors, you've undoubtedly heard about "instructor burn-out." This very real malady is often faced by pilots who have been instructing intensively for one to two years or more. Most commonly it afflicts the types of instructors we discussed earlier: those just "passing through" on their way up the career ladder. Interestingly enough, pilots who've been instructing for many years and plan to keep doing so are less-often victims of burn-out.

Obviously those long-time instructors like what they're doing well enough to stay with it, so they're less likely to get sick of it. But there's another factor. Long-time instructors generally have learned the stress-reducing benefits of being selective in choosing their students. Instructing is heck of a lot more fun when you stick with students who prepare well for their lessons, show good judgment, and are a pleasure to work with. New CFIs are delighted to take on whatever students they can get. But watch the more senior instructors; you'll see that they filter their students very carefully. It's yet another benefit of having plenty of students to choose from.

The moral of this story is that to be really successful, most instructors benefit by doing a certain amount of student recruiting themselves. At every flight school there are a few instructors who have all the work they can handle, even if everyone else is slow. There's a good reason for that; the go-getters line up their own students, and arrange to have more waiting in the wings. That's where you want to be.

Now back to the original question: "Why do I need to line up my own flight students?" Because it will help you get a CFI job, increase your flying and income while you're doing it, and open up other professional piloting opportunities for the future. Good reasons, wouldn't you say? We'll delve into the details of how to do this in the next chapter.

TYPES OF INSTRUCTING POSITIONS

Given that flight training requirements are so clearly defined by federal regulation, it's interesting that specific CFI jobs can vary so much in character. Among the most common instructor employers are airline "ab initio" programs (see below), universities, large private flight training schools, and private FBOs. Each type of position offers its own advantages and disadvantages for instructors, so the decision of which is best for each pilot must be based on personality and professional objectives.

Contract Ab Initio Programs

Many foreign airlines and several U.S. regional carriers operate their own "ab initio" flight training programs. *Ab initio* means "from the beginning," and refers to programs which students enter with no prior experience. Each student is trained from his or her first flight lesson through all of the ratings, and up to entry-level qualifications established by the contracting (or operating) carrier. These programs are sometimes run by the foreign carrier itself, and in other cases operated under contract by American flight schools. U.S. programs are generally located in Florida, the Southwest, and California, where the weather is favorable for efficient flight training.

Ab initio programs tend to be very regimented, since the object is to move large numbers of students through the program quickly and with good standardization. The result can be a rather high-pressure instructing environment. Training schedules must be rigidly adhered to, so long work days are sometimes required to keep all of the students "on track." Each lesson is highly structured, so there's a good deal of repetition. Procedures and performance standards are established by the affiliated carrier, and are often different from those of the FAA. For instructors, these differences mean extra study, but they often benefit by learning multi-pilot crew coordination more thoroughly than in other instructional settings.

The foreign carrier ab initio programs generally pay very well for CFI positions. One can build flight experience rapidly, the equipment is generally first class, and opportunities often exist to move up into twins and even turboprop aircraft. The flipside to this is these outfits generally require their new hires to have 2,000–2,500 hours of flight instructing experience; plus, a year or more of single-engine primary instruction may be required of new CFIs before they can move into larger aircraft.

Opportunities for making career contacts at these sorts of places are usually limited to affiliated airlines. Since most foreign airlines hire only their own nationals, American CFI employees may need to network outside such schools for truly useful contacts.

If you're the kind of person who prefers a regimented job with clearly defined work parameters, those bigger airline flight schools are probably for you. Since they tend to be rigorous on scheduling, the ab initio programs are ideal for instructors who prefer to work very hard for a fairly regular shift at normal hours, and then go home.

University Flight Programs and Large Private Flight Schools

Universities and big-name private flight schools also offer top-notch instructing experience in which one can build time rapidly. These programs are also quite structured, and have the same scheduling and standardization pressures as the airline schools, but with less pay. There's a good deal of prestige associated with such outfits, however, and the large number of graduates can later provide their instructors with excellent career contacts around the country and even around the world.

University programs tend to be a little more democratic in operation than the big private flight schools. Research opportunities sometimes arise in the course of instructing, and there tends to be more interest in experimenting with new teaching methods.

A potential benefit of instructing at university programs is the prestige of teaching at an institution of higher learning. Although teaching at a major university may not be so different than what goes on at the private flight school down the road, it has far more cachet on a resume. A year or two later when you apply for your next flying job, you'll have impressive experience to show for it.

FBOs and Smaller Private Flight Schools

FBOs and smaller private flight schools are much more variable in the ways they operate, and therefore in the opportunities they offer their instructors. There is generally less flying (but not always) at such outfits, and often less money than at the big flight schools.

The good news is that in many cases a good FBO employee can look forward to moving up quickly into bigger equipment in the charter department. In addition there also tends to be more interaction by flight instructors with the outside aviation community than at larger outfits, so the prospects of making career contacts in the course of the job are excellent. It's also more likely at an FBO that some of your students will ultimately offer additional flying and career opportunities.

As one might imagine, small to mid-sized private flight schools are ideal for the entrepreneur, since they tend to operate in a more free-wheeling manner than the bigger outfits. Sales skills for student recruiting are especially important for CFIs at FBOs, as is flexibility in performing tasks in addition to instructing itself. And FBO instructors tend to operate with greater independence and more personal responsibility than their counterparts at the big schools.

CHOOSING THE RIGHT FLIGHT SCHOOL TO WORK FOR

Along with type of training environment, there are other factors to consider as you shop for employers. A disappointing number of aviation businesses are poorly managed. You'll want to work for an outfit that strives for excellence, particularly in the way it treats its customers and employees. If others you meet at the flight school are unhappy, you probably will be, too.

It's also helpful to keep your eyes peeled for flight operations which are much busier than others in the same area. Reasons why one outfit is busy while another is slow aren't always apparent on the surface, but they often boil down to how they handle basic business practices such as marketing, personnel management, and customer service.

Take the time to size up the management at flight schools that interest you, and to interview a few instructors and customers on the ramp. If you don't like what you hear, you're probably wisest to avoid the place, even if they do offer you a job. Always, the best job-hunting objective is to pursue positions at the really outstanding outfits—even if it takes a bit longer.

Other particularly important points to look for: is your potential employer aggressive about pursuing students? How well do they treat their customers once they've got them? These issues are critically important to you, even if you're in the "part-time-drum-up-your-own" category. If the flight school markets aggressively, they'll appreciate, support and encourage your efforts to attract students. Also, no matter how great your instructing may be, you'll be hard-pressed to make up for poor customer service elsewhere in the company. You're in this business to deliver a professional service to your flight students. Working for a company with poor customer relations means less work for you, less professional fulfillment, and far less satisfaction for your customers.

A related issue is the organization and management of the flight training program itself. The really good flight schools have well-organized flight training programs taught by syllabus, with built-in and careful monitoring of student progress. Not only will your students benefit by such a program, but so will you. Half the battle in developing your own professionalism is finding a place to work where you'll learn something. Ideally it will be the kind of outfit where you'll grow a great deal professionally, learning from both the more experienced instructors and through the guidance of a rigorous training program.

So shop around a bit before signing on for your first instructing job. Look for an outfit that will encourage, support, and appreciate you and your students. Not only will you have more fun there, but your students will enjoy their training more, and you'll benefit from being associated with a flight school having a good reputation.

ON YOUR OWN: INDEPENDENT FLIGHT INSTRUCTORS

A good many CFIs practice in the broad category of independent flight instructors, which includes everyone from self-employed "freelancers," to flight school part-timers who line up their own students.

Perhaps the most obvious independent flight instructors are those who are self-employed. Many of these CFIs promote their services to aircraft owners, offering checkouts in aircraft new to them, advanced ratings, and recurrent training such as flight reviews and instrument proficiency checks. Other independents offer flight training in aircraft they own themselves, sometimes with a professional objective such as building multi-engine time in a personally owned twin.

As you might suspect, making a full-time living as a self-employed flight instructor can be challenging; it requires a sales-oriented personality, an established reputation, and perhaps most importantly, a busy aviation location. Some self-employed instructors find it valuable to affiliate with flying clubs. Larger clubs, especially those allowing primary training in their aircraft, can sometimes keep one or more instructors busy pretty much full time. Other independent CFIs limit their instructing to part time "on the side," while working a regular, non-flying job at the same time.

Freelancers must carefully address business and legal matters, such as carrying adequate liability insurance, and ensuring that the local airport doesn't prohibit freelance flight instruction. As you would expect, freelancers are often people who enjoy being in business for themselves; sometimes it's also possible for them to set and collect higher hourly fees than they could as employees.

Odd as it may sound, the largest number of independent CFIs can probably be found on the payroll at local flight schools. Part-time instructors, including the new CFIs mentioned earlier in this chapter, often line up their own students and set their own schedules, but deliver and bill their services through the flight school. These independent employees enjoy the benefits of affiliation with the flight school, including access to aircraft, facilities, and potential students, but must do their own marketing and manage their affairs, much like a self-employed instructor. Even "full-time" flight school instructors sometimes find themselves scrambling for business like their independent counterparts, when times are slow.

Flight instructors share many common opportunities and challenges when it comes to keeping their instructing schedules full. In that respect there's a bit of "independent flight instructor" in most CFIs, whether self-employed or not.

THREE

Where Do New Students Come From?

Despite rumors to the contrary, there are still plenty of aspiring pilots out there. The problem is not all of them are aggressive or confident enough, for various reasons, to come out to the airport and sign up for lessons. Some know they want to become pilots, others have not yet caught the "bug" but would, if exposed.

The trigger, for most of those would-be pilots, is meeting the right instructor. Once they've identified an expert they like and trust, and perhaps had a few nagging questions answered, they'll get started on those long-postponed flying lessons. Many of your best recruiting opportunities will be meeting these closet pilots at their earliest stages of interest. Catch them before they've initiated their own trip to the airport, and you'll gain a new student.

In this chapter we're going to talk about how and where to attract prospective flight students from outside of your flight school office. In the upcoming chapters we'll examine how to "close the deal" by signing them up.

TYPES OF FLIGHT STUDENTS

Most of your prospective clients fall into a few fairly well-defined categories: those who plan to fly professionally, those interested in using airplanes for personal business travel, and those who desire to fly strictly for recreation. While the methods we discuss should help to attract all types of fliers, it's important to understand a few of the basic differences between them.

Aspiring Professional Pilots

For our purposes here, professional pilots are those who want to make permanent, full-time careers out of flying. Of course, as CFIs we want to teach every student to *fly* like a professional, even if it's in a Piper Cub on weekends. But most aspiring pros hope to ultimately fly big jets for a major airline, or smaller jets for a good corporate employer. Many also seek flying careers with the military.

There are several different avenues which these students can take for their training. Many career-oriented young people enroll in university professional programs, such as Purdue, Embry-Riddle, and the University of North Dakota, or in one of the big private flight schools such as Flight Safety International, or Comair Academy.

For instructors doing their own recruiting, students considering the big schools are usually not the best prospects. The big flight programs support themselves through massive, specialized national or international marketing—not something an individual can effectively compete with. Rather, for most CFIs the best pro-pilot candidates will be those who, for whatever reason, wish to remain in the immediate community to complete their flight training. Likely prospects in this category include students transitioning into flying from another career, those who must work full time and earn a living while training, those in school studying some other major, and those with family obligations.

There are a number of positive aspects to instructing career-oriented students. They tend to be fairly serious about their studies, and usually have a budget plan designed to get them through each rating, sometimes even pre-paid. Since career-track students want to get through their training promptly, they tend to schedule more frequent lessons than other students. They're also more likely to fly on weekdays, an otherwise slow time for many instructors.

The benefits of instructing these folks are steadier flying and income for you, and more serious students (most of the time) who will return for multiple ratings. You'll build hours more quickly with aspiring pros than with other students, but the flying tends to be more regimented.

Business Fliers

Your next group of prospective clients includes successful professional and business people from outside aviation, who feel that piloting a personal airplane would benefit them in pursuit of business success. These folks tend to be excellent prospects in that they usually have money and want to complete the training in a prompt but thorough manner. They often incorporate some business travel into their lessons, which means more flying variety, income, and experience for you. And if the training goes well, business types often return for additional ratings.

The best news for you is that business fliers have money and contacts. When the lessons are over they often buy airplanes. Guess who gets called first to fly them? Their trusted old instructors, of course!

And these students have connections. They are frequently in a position to steer their instructors to other professional flying opportunities, if they were impressed by the training.

On the other hand, successful entrepreneurs and business professionals tend to have a high degree of self-confidence ("ego" as some would call it). This means you've got to be very careful to retain the respect of such students, and to maintain positive control over the training program. Don't let them forget who's the instructor.

Pleasure Pilots

Among the greatest recruiting opportunities for CFIs these days are pleasure fliers, recreational pilots who choose to fly strictly for the fun of it. The economy is strong, and people are routinely taking on leisure-time activities equaling or exceeding the investment level of flying. Skiing, golfing, boating—you name the expensive hobby and people are out there in droves enjoying it.

With the ongoing revitalization of the general aviation industry, exciting new education and recruiting programs are once again trumpeting the joys of flying to the public. Primary training airplanes are again being manufactured in quantity, and new light aircraft models are once more being introduced. In short, the winds are blowing in our favor for recruiting of pleasure pilots.

Unfortunately pleasure flying has not, over the past few years, been growing at the rate of other leisure-time activities like those mentioned above, and it's worth taking a moment to consider why. As light aircraft manufacturing and flight training declined during the 1980s and early '90s, organized efforts to attract recreational pilots fell largely by the wayside. The problem was compounded because as pleasure flying declined, the public had less exposure to small airplanes than previously. Since fewer people were flying for pleasure, their neighbors and friends no longer got the opportunity to go for a plane ride, either.

For these reasons, public familiarity with the pleasure, utility, and personal satisfaction of flying is probably on the lowest level it's been in many years. There are more pleasure pilot prospects out there than ever, but they're a bit harder to find than they used to be. That means more work for you in educating your prospects, but given today's more aggressive industry climate, it also means greater opportunity.

We as flight instructors are ideally positioned to recruit new pleasure pilots, because educating people about the joys of flying is our profession. And no one knows better than you that once hooked, the dream of flight never goes away.

You'll find that pleasure pilots get joy out of flying like few others, and that they tend to lean harder on their instructors as professionals. Pleasure pilots aren't called "weekend pilots" for nothing. Many work during the week and will require their lessons on weekends. They're also more likely get busy periodically, or to have to conform to a budget. As a result their flying tends to be less frequent and not as consistent as with the other two groups we've discussed.

In certain respects, pleasure fliers offer the best prospects for a new instructor. You're more likely to find these folks among your casual acquaintances, and if they already know you the sales effort to enroll them is usually minimal. Every one of us knows someone who wishes they could fly. It's just a matter of identifying who these folks are, and getting them out to the airport!

WHERE AND HOW TO MEET PROSPECTIVE FLIGHT STUDENTS

Now that we've set the stage, we're ready to talk about techniques for attracting prospective flight students. As an individual, your marketing efforts will be most effective in drawing flight students from the geographic area in which you instruct. Therefore, it's at the flight schools with a local or regional business base where personal recruiting efforts work best. With that in mind, the focus on recruiting in this section will be primarily upon your local community.

The good news is that besides those big flight schools mentioned earlier, flight instruction is generally poorly marketed, if at all. So there's no need to run a TV commercial during the Super Bowl to blow away the competition. With work and a little creativity, it's possible to market your services very effectively with minimal cash investment.

Although they're interrelated, the marketing tools for building your flight instruction business fall loosely into two categories: traditional sales methods, and networking.

To the uninitiated, traditional tools like advertising and direct mail always seem the best to do because they're, well, *traditional*. Those methods probably do work best for sales of commodity products. Customers see an ad, go to the store, and hopefully buy the products.

But flight instruction is more like the professional services offered by doctors, accountants, and attorneys. Service professionals build most of their business through *networking* (some call it "word of mouth"). For anyone promoting a consulting service such as flying lessons, it's hard to beat networking for effectiveness.

With that in mind, let's start off with the networking methods, and then work our way into the more traditional methods. Remember, while any one marketing method alone may work, most sales professionals recommend using a combination of several techniques simultaneously.

Networking Activities

If you talk to independent professionals such as accountants, dentists and attorneys, and to service-types such as financial consultants and insurance people, you'll find most of them are heavily involved in community activities. Hopefully their involvement is due to a sense of civic responsibility, but you can bet that another objective is marketing. In the course of working with lots of people in the community, those consultants and professionals get to know folks who are prospects for their services. The more people they meet, the better. And that approach works just as well for selling flight lessons.

Work the Aviation Events

As a logical starting point, you'll want to volunteer for public contact duties at aviation activities that many of your prospects are likely to attend.

Sign up as a docent or tour guide at a nearby aviation museum. Your job there will be explaining airplanes to visitors who are intrigued with flight. Think any of them might be interested in lessons? A growing number of museums offer after-hours opportunities, too. Along with various fundraising events, many rent their facilities to companies and community groups for banquets and parties. Those kinds of events are great places to make contacts, if you're in the right volunteer position.

Airshows are also great, because they draw such huge crowds. Somebody must be interested in flying, because according to the Aircraft Owners and Pilots Association (AOPA), when it comes to major public events, air show attendance is surpassed only by major league baseball!

Airport open houses and pancake fly-ins in smaller communities present excellent opportunities since they, too, attract the general public. Obviously, you're far better off working the information booth or the grandstand than directing traffic in the parking lot. The objective, after all, is to personally interact with as many people as you can.

Another option is to set up your own booth. Construct a nice professional-looking sign, and make yourself available to answer questions about the event, about flying, and about airplanes. Ask your flight school to cover the cost of the booth. No dice? If necessary, split cost and time in the booth with other instructors; there should be plenty of business for everybody. (More about hand-out materials for these events later in this chapter.)

A great place to learn about regional aviation activities like those we've just discussed is through your local chapter of the Experimental Aircraft Association. Not only do local EAA chapters host many of those events, but they also promote learning to fly in their communities through a program called "Flying Start." Think they could use an instructor?

Of course you'll want to attend any and all aviation community events—FAA Safety Seminars, for example. Already-licensed pilots periodically seek instruction, too. Not only are there new ratings to pursue, but also refresher training opportunities such as the FAA's Wings proficiency program, flight reviews, and instrument competency checks.

Just about any local pilot organization offers instructing opportunities. Joining a member-owned flying club opens access to a ready supply of pilots who can use your services. In fact, many flying clubs designate "Club CFIs," who act as training and safety advisors while enjoying special instructing privileges within the club.

It's simple: the more visible you are as an instructor in the aviation community, the greater the demand will be for your services.

Volunteer for Community Service and Charities

The great thing about volunteer work is the opportunity to build your business in the course of helping some worthy organization. While aviation activities can introduce you to a specifically qualified group of potential students, volunteering for other causes can be just as rewarding. Everyone benefits by putting energy back into their community.

Sign up for causes you believe in, where there is plenty of involvement by successful community members. Volunteer to work for your church, for community service groups such as Lions and Kiwanis, or for fund-raising charities like United Way and the Heart Association. Your local chamber of commerce and community business organizations also appreciate volunteers. Community business fairs and chamber of commerce trade shows can also be great places to set up a booth.

The key to networking in any charitable or business organization is to get involved in committee work. That's where you'll meet successful people who can afford to learn to fly, if they're interested. Outreach committees like membership and fund-raising are best because they offer opportunities to meet people both inside and outside the organization.

"Wait a minute," you say, "I can't be out there soliciting flight students at church functions!" True, it may not be appropriate to distribute "Learn to Fly" brochures at the annual charity ball, but you will get the chance to talk with lots of people there. And one question almost everyone asks is "What do you do for a living?" It'll quickly become apparent who might be interested in flying lessons. Just ask for a phone number and call later to answer their questions, when the time is right for talking airplanes.

Your Role As Teacher

Always remember that most prospective students are a bit apprehensive about flying, no matter how great their interest, and no matter how confident they may appear. To most people flying still seems difficult and dangerous. All but the most confident prospects will wait to start lessons until they meet someone they know and trust.

Your objective, then, is to meet students while in your role as a professional and an expert. There's no better way to fill that role than teaching. Do a good job in the classroom, and your ground school students will recognize you as an expert whom they know personally. They'll beg you to take them on as flight students!

Offer Learn-to-Fly Seminars

Many people who are interested in learning to fly don't know much about it. One way to address that group is to offer an "Introduction To Flying" course at your flight school. Select a time when many people would be available to attend, send an announcement to the "community events" section of your local newspaper, scour the presentation room spotlessly clean, and order some simple refreshments.

The trick with introductory presentations is to emphasize the *benefits* of becoming a pilot, and to keep discussion about the process as non-technical as possible. Of course it's important that your guests see the airplanes (which should be spotless too), tour the rest of your facility, and meet other flight school employees in the process.

Your objective must go beyond informing your audience, in order to generate a good return from the course. As part of the seminar you should offer some "tonight-only" incentives for attendees to enroll right away in lessons. This could be as simple as a free or discounted first lesson coupon, but the better plan is to offer incentives that go beyond one lesson, like a ground school enrollment discount, or a solo package special. You might even consider a creative twist on that first lesson deal, like giving the fifth lesson free. That provides you with several additional lessons to get your prospects really hooked on flight.

Teach Aviation Ground Schools

Sign up to teach private and instrument pilot ground schools at your flight school whenever possible. It is often the case that getting a ground school teaching opportunity is not too difficult, since most CFIs don't want to take on non-flying activities. If your flight school doesn't offer ground schools, offer to set one up. (Your boss may be concerned that attendance could be too low to cover your pay; if so, offer to work for a percentage of the door receipts.)

Someone's already teaching the evening ground school? Volunteer to attend as an assistant; aid the teacher in answering questions and helping students to solve problems. Either way, students will get to know you in the role of expert.

As we've discussed, many licensed pilots are prospects for refresher instruction and new ratings. Along with certificate-oriented ground schools, offer Flight Review and Instrument Competency Refresher classes. (Instrument students are particularly desirable because they'll keep you sharp for that interview simulator ride you'll be taking one of these days.)

Next, there are seminars. Most of us tend to think of classroom instruction strictly in the context of specific ratings. But there are also opportunities to offer one- or two-session seminar-type courses covering specialized topics, to your flying community. Seminars serve the dual purposes of educating people and marketing your instructing services.

Among possible topics: local weather hazards, mountain flying, and introduction to advanced aircraft rented by your flight school. A particularly hot pilot topic now is practical use of GPS, the Global Positioning System.

We've already mentioned an introductory what-it's-all-about "Learn to Fly" course. Then there's "Introduction to Instrument Flying for Private Pilots," and "Principles of Aerobatics." Interested in any multi-engine students? How about a "Multi-Engine Basics" ground school?

With seminars, attendance can vary tremendously based on topic, pricing, day of the week, and dumb luck. One seminar may be packed and the next unattended. (Be prepared to eat all of those chocolate-chip cookies yourself!) Rather than offering just one seminar to see if it works, it's wisest to test the concept through a series. Plan several on a regular schedule, promote them, and see them through.

Finally, contact the national companies who offer weekend ground school programs around the country. They promote their offerings aggressively, and support their teachers with professionally-prepared course presentation materials. Most use local instructors, in each city where the course is offered, to teach a heavily-marketed weekend ground school every few months. If selected, you'll be paid well (by flight instructor standards), and many attendees will be new prospects for flight training whom you wouldn't otherwise meet.

Community College Courses

Flight schools are not the only places where aviation topics are taught. Many community colleges offer introductory pilot ground school courses in their continuing education catalogs. Approach these institutions about teaching their courses. Be sure to check the qualifications; you may need to apply for a community college teaching certificate ahead of time.

If there is no course, offer to set one up. Usually community college "night school" courses are approved simply based on having a qualified instructor and some minimum number of students.

The great thing about teaching at community colleges is that most do not offer the flight training portion. Think about it, you're an aviation expert standing in front of ten, twenty or more ground school students, each of them wondering how and where to start flying!

Here again, if someone else is already scheduled to instruct the course, call the teacher and volunteer to work as an unpaid assistant. If there are more than a few people in the class the instructor is going to have his or her hands full answering questions. Your help will be especially appreciated during the more labor-intensive sections, like cross-country planning.

If all else fails, sign up for the course and attend it yourself. Make it clear early in the course (and in a diplomatic manner) that you're a CFI, and that you're attending the class in order to keep your own knowledge sharp. Ask good questions and make useful comments. Offer your services to the teacher in helping other students with questions. Soon, other students will be quizzing you after class about how, when and where they should start flying.

The continuing education courses we've discussed so far address the FAA Knowledge Exams for specific pilot ratings. They're generally found in the "for-credit" catalog. But there's an additional category of classes to consider: Have you ever noticed all of those "non-credit" classes offered through your local community college? Ever considered where they come from? In most places, anyone can propose a non-credit course to teach for their community college. (For non-credit courses, your CFI certificate should be all the qualification you'll need.) You'll have to come up with a good course concept, as with last section's seminar topics, then "sell" the idea to the community college. Their primary interest will be in the number of attendees you can attract. There's not much money in teaching the courses themselves, but the real issue is — can you attract any students?

Meet Prospects at Work

If you're like so many other impoverished pilots, you may need to work another job while getting your instructing off the ground. This can be a great marketing opportunity if you take a position where you'll meet prospective students.

It's always interesting to see how many fliers feel that, in order to become professional pilots, they must immediately quit their other jobs and hang out at the airport. Yet for most instructors, working at a job outside of aviation is a great way to line up students. (It also pays the bills!) Large companies, for example, offer all sorts of opportunities to spread the word, and even to directly solicit students. Company newsletters and bulletin boards target gainfully employed people who can afford to fly. Post some airplane pictures around your cubicle and see if anybody notices.

For those already instructing full time, consider spending some of your "free-time" at a job where you'll line up some students. Anywhere successful local people hang out is a good place to work. Take a job as a waiter or a bartender at a fine restaurant frequented by successful, in-town people. Busier country clubs and golf courses are good spots to caddie or work in the pro shop.

These are all places where you can make good money while meeting lots of successful people. Sure, not everyone is going to be a prospect, and with most patrons the topic of airplanes will never come up. But if you do a good job at work, it's surprising how many people will chat with you about your "other" life. Many of the regulars will get to know you by name, and next thing you know, they'll be referring students.

The numbers alone give you great odds, as long as you work in a place with plenty of traffic. If one in a hundred customers has a connection and takes the time to talk to you, you should be able to line up a student or two a week.

Skeptical? Let me tell you about Dave, who worked as a waiter and bartender at a good restaurant for two years, while earning his CFI and then instructing.

"I could have flown an unlimited amount," he told me, "based just on people I met at the restaurant." Along with flying plenty of demonstration rides, Dave lined up six flight students for himself, and made about a dozen contacts who directly resulted in his logging of over a hundred hours of multi-engine time. "I lined up more students at the restaurant than I could handle, so I had to trade a lot of them to other instructors," Dave told me. Ultimately he landed a Cessna 310 pilot position with one of his regular customers.

I asked Dave how he'd spread the word. "I never forgot why I was there," he told me. "Whenever I went to work I wasn't a waiter, or a bartender; I was a pilot. When people asked I told them 'I'm a pilot doing this temporarily.'" In fact, one of Dave's first acts after being hired had been to take the restaurant manager flying. "Pretty soon everyone who came in knew I was 'that pilot who works here.'"

"Dave," I said, "you are amazing—wasn't there *any* downside to working at the restaurant?"

"Well," he replied, "I was a little disappointed that I didn't get the King Air job I was working on with one of the customers."

Wear Your Profession On Your Sleeve

By now you should be asking yourself, "Gee whiz! How can I possibly talk with enough people in all these places to find out who's interested in flying?" The answer is incredibly simple. You don't have to *talk* with everybody. At aviation events wear a flight suit, epaulets, and/or some flying wings. Your prospects will be thrilled at the opportunity to meet a "real" professional pilot, as long as they can identify you as one. But don't stop there.

Always wear something aviation-related, wherever you go. While you're doing your volunteer work, playing a round of golf, out for dinner at a restaurant, or even in the driveway washing your car, others will know you're a pilot. Just wearing something flying-oriented shows that you're proud of your career, and you're approachable about it. T-shirts, hats, ties, and even tie tacks are noticed by those who care. Wear an aviation watch.

Think anyone will notice your "jet jockey" T-shirt? You bet! If anyone around is interested in flying, you'll be cornered in minutes. Current and aspiring pilots will approach you, along with other aviation enthusiasts of all varieties. Even "friends of pilots" will want to speak with you!

Don't feel that you have to wear the Cessna 152 you instruct in. A big part of flying, for most of us, is the dream. Show off any aircraft you like. All that matters is letting others know you like airplanes.

Even when working other jobs it's usually possible to discreetly display your profession. As a bartender or golf caddie, you may be able to wear a playful aviation tie or shirt. On uniforms and suits, aviation tie tacks and lapel pins are noticed far more often than you think.

The point is that in order to attract students, you need to let everyone know you're a pilot, not hide it. And *the further away from the airport you get, the more important it is to wear your profession on your sleeve*, or your lapel, your tie, wherever you can show it off. If someone is interested in learning to fly and is already at the airport, you may be faced with a little friendly competition.

But if someone at the swimming pool asks you about your "Lucky Lindy" bathing trunks, odds are pretty good that you're the only aviation expert around. Now that you know they're interested, you've got a new prospect — even if your business cards *are* all wet!

Promotional Paperwork: Tools of the Trade

Speaking of business cards, let's delve into what types of promotional paperwork are required in order to accomplish what we've been talking about. When customers consider purchasing professional services like flying lessons, there are certain standards they expect, such as professional-quality business cards, and printed materials which explain, qualify, and give credibility to their bearers.

Business Cards

Business cards are important to carry for a number of reasons. First, when properly executed they present you as a professional in your field. Next, cards allow you to provide your credentials and contact information in a concise manner. (In other words, you won't have to borrow a crayon and a napkin.) Business cards can also serve to remind your contact a little about you as a person, long after your meeting.

Everybody knows what a business card should look like, right? Just run down to the quick-print shop, select a design with a little airplane on it, print it on the cheapest white card stock they've got, and pick it up tomorrow for $35.

Bad idea! Plain white cards are only a good idea if (1) you want to look like everyone else, (2) you don't want to give anyone the impression that flying might be fun, and (3) you want to convey the message that you'll probably be in business for only about a week.

What you are selling to prospective pilots is excitement, adventure, and fun (more on this in upcoming chapters), so that's what you want to convey on your business cards. The best way to do that is with a smashing color photo! Photo business cards are among the most valuable but under-used promotional tools available. They are simply business cards that incorporate a picture in the design—possibly with you in it, but definitely with an airplane.

Photo business cards are great for networking because they improve your luck: Every time you swap cards it's instantly clear that you're a pilot—not a word needs to be said. As a result, photo business cards are ideal for handing out to all those people you meet who never really considered flying, but might be interested if they knew more about it. And there you are to answer their questions! With a photo business card you don't even have to mention that you're a flight instructor; if the person receiving your card is even the slightest bit interested in flying, or knows someone who is, you're going to hear about it.

Why won't a card with a logo do the same thing? Because your objective is to hand everyone a card, and then they see a Cherokee soaring over the

Red Rocks of Sedona, Arizona at sunset, and exclaim, "Cool! You mean you actually fly airplanes? I have *always* wanted to do that!" And with every note you write, and every time a prospect flips by your business card in a card file, someone will be reminded of just how "cool" flying is, and that you're the lucky individual who teaches people how to do it.

Photo business cards are commonly produced using one of two methods, photographic reproduction or four-color (meaning "full color") offset printing. Photographic versions are printed on photo paper and are available through photo-finishers, while offset-printed business cards are produced by printing companies.

Traditionally more expensive than those produced by photo-finishers, offset-printed cards are of higher and more lasting quality. (It'll take some shopping, but four-color offset business cards are now available from some sources for as little as $100 per thousand cards.)

If you absolutely cannot afford to go with color, ask your local quick-print outfit to "screen" your photo, and then print it as part of a one- or two-color business card. (They'll know how to do it, and the cost will be only seven to ten dollars more than a basic logo card.) As soon as they're printed, *start using those cards!*

Regardless of the type of business card you choose, keep in mind that the photo must be excellent, to make it really effective. Also, a business card is one of the few stationery items you can have fun with. For example, while you may wish to dress up in a flight shirt and tie for your business card photo, you might also consider one in casual dress next to a hobby aircraft like glider, warbird, or antique.

By the way, having those exciting new business cards in hand will strike you with the irresistible urge to hand them to everyone you meet. But remember, with prospective students, hand over your card only *after* collecting theirs. That way you can follow up with them later.

Brochures and Other Promotional Materials

Brochures are important marketing tools for flight training, partly because the benefits and process of earning a pilot certificate often require more explanation than can easily be addressed in a casual meeting.

There are ideally three objectives with promotional materials for selling flying. First and foremost, the objective is to convey the adventure and benefits of being a pilot. Second, the material should explain just enough about airplanes and flying to stimulate prospects' interest so they will want to talk more with you. Third, the promo material qualifies the expertise of instructor or flight school, as appropriate.

Producing original materials to do these things can be expensive; they're feasible for large flight schools, but are likely out of reach for individual instructors and smaller outfits. However, a number of industry organizations produce wonderful learn-to-fly materials which you can use to promote aviation.[1] Many are designed to be personalized using adhesive labels or rubber stamps.

The best ways to use such materials are not always what one would expect. Rather than giving away your best brochures to every interested prospect you meet, the better plan is to use them as tools for the specific purpose of developing an ongoing relationship with your prospect. When you meet prospective pilots at the airshow, you want to create another opportunity to talk to them, hopefully over an introductory flight lesson at the airport. But very often anything you hand away at that moment is going to hit the trash, or at best end up in a file folder somewhere, long before your new contact ever gets around to calling you.

So the proper approach is to start by offering to send your new-found prospects information on flying. Then you can collect their addresses and phone numbers for future follow-up. Having done that, hand them your business card, and if you're at an airshow or trade show booth, a basic flyer to get them started.

---

[1]Among them are AOPA (Aircraft Owners and Pilots Association), GA Team 2000, *Flight Training* magazine, NATA (National Air Transportation Association), GAMA (General Aviation Manufacturers Association, EAA (Experimental Aircraft Association), and NAFI (National Association of Flight Instructors).

Next, mail each prospect a nice brochure covering the adventure and benefits of being a pilot, along with your card and a personal letter inviting them out to the airport for an introductory flight. Then follow up the introductory flight with a phone call to answer any questions they may have, and invite them once again. Even if they're not yet ready to start, you now have a qualified prospect you can develop over time.

Go Public

Another good way to attract students is to publicly become a general aviation advocate. That means representing the general aviation community in every way possible.

Solicit Media Coverage

Have you ever wondered where the community and feature articles in your local newspaper come from? Sure, when the bowling alley burns down, the paper automatically sends a reporter over to cover it. But most of the less urgent material comes from the newsmakers themselves, often with the help of a public relations, or "P.R." consultant.

If you're willing to make the effort, you can accomplish some pretty effective P.R. yourself. The objective is to generate continuing news coverage of your instructional activities in the local media. At the least, you should be able to make the "community events" and "people" pages on a regular basis. If you're lucky and do a good job of staying in touch, you may also be able to periodically stimulate feature coverage in the form of major newspaper articles, TV stories, and radio interviews.

The first step in your P.R. plan is to prepare a standard "News Release" form. This can be as simple as a piece of your business letterhead, incorporating your logo and contact information with the words, "News Release" prominently displayed across the top. Whenever you can come up with any interesting aviation events, accomplishments or activities, type up a brief but catchy description on one of your News Release forms. Duplicate it and fax or mail copies to each of the local papers, TV and radio stations.

What merits a news release? Ground schools of all varieties and "Introduction To Flying" classes can almost always be listed for free in local newspapers, as long as you submit the information well in advance.

First solos, newly earned pilot certificates, and other piloting achievements of your students can also be newsworthy. In these cases your news release should include some interesting facts about each student, such as his or her profession, and perhaps a quote about why he or she is learning to fly. (Be sure to get your students' permission on the content! Have them "okay" and initial your copy of the news release before sending it away.)

Along with naming your student's accomplishment, be sure to explain what it means and why it's important. Of course, every news release should prominently feature your name, as instructor, and the name and location of your flight school.

Take a look at the text of a sample news release in the following illustration on the next page.

Notice that adding background about the student's professional activities has contributed to the newsworthiness of her flying achievement. It also takes advantage of her flying objectives to present some benefits of being a pilot which might interest other prospects.

To add further pizzazz to your news releases, carry a camera loaded with black and white film in your flight bag, and use it to photograph your students and newsworthy aviation events. Newspaper editors love to use photos, whenever possible. Newspapers print most of their photos in black and white, and they always look better when reproduced from good black and white originals. Since relatively few news releases arrive with photos, especially in black and white, you've got an edge of opportunity if yours do include them. Send in a nice black and white snapshot with every news release, and there's a very good chance that some grateful editor will print both story and picture.

F. Light Training, Inc.
15505 Highway 4 • Cityville, VT 00221 • (123) 645–3219

********* **NEWS RELEASE** *********

LOCAL PHYSICIAN PILOTS AIRPLANE
TO FIRST SOLO FLIGHT

(b&w photos enclosed)

Prominent local pediatrician Dr. Mary Woodfly, yesterday accomplished her first solo flight as pilot of an airplane, at Cityville Municipal Airport.

Dr. Woodfly, well-known in the community for her work with diabetic children, has been taking flying lessons from Certified Flight Instructor Marva Loos, for the last six weeks. Family members videotaped the first flight, which was followed by a traditional "first solo" celebration at the F. Light Training facility, located on the south side of the airport off Highway 4.

Asked to describe her experience afterwards, Dr. Woodfly flashed a victory sign and said, "This is an incredible day for me, the first step in my life-long dream of becoming a pilot. I just wish I'd done this twenty years sooner!"

Upon completing her training, Dr. Woodfly plans to use her Private Pilot certificate both for family pleasure travel, and to serve Cityville Clinic's new location at Mt. Pleasant, which is projected to open later this summer. Dr. Woodfly initially plans to rent airplanes at F. Light Training, Inc., and then eventually to buy her own plane.

For more information, please contact Fred Light, of F. Light Training Enterprises at the above telephone number, or Dr. Mary Woodfly at Cityville Clinic, 645-4412.

F. Light Training, helping people fly their dreams for over thirty years.

Consistent news coverage serves several useful purposes in attracting new students. First, it gets your name and that of your flight school into the paper where prospective pilots can see them, hopefully on a regular basis. News coverage is free, and often more eye-catching than the level of advertising most of us can afford to pay for.

Secondly, news coverage gets your students some attention. Friends and associates will see them featured and grill them about it—"Hey, I didn't know you're taking flying lessons; what's the story?" It's particularly valuable to showcase the flying activities of community professionals and business people; the more varied types of people shown flying airplanes, the better for general aviation's basic reputation in the public eye.

Yet another benefit of regular news coverage is personal recognition for you as an aviation professional, by media staff. Hopefully they'll think of you and call for an interview in some flying-related story. But don't be afraid to make the first move yourself. Is there a big aviation event coming up at your local airfield? Call your local media well in advance to let them know what's happening, and to make yourself available for an interview at the event. Is there a local airport organization with which you can serve? That's potentially newsworthy, too, and would certainly identify you as an expert. Another good angle is to invite a newspaper, TV, or radio reporter for an introductory flying lesson. (AOPA has some excellent reference materials on how best to do this.) If a story results, you'll be the subject!

Make Yourself Available for Speaking Engagements

Have you ever considered just how many community organizations have meetings every month? Along with the Chamber of Commerce, Lions and Kiwanis Clubs, there are church, charitable and civic groups, men's and women's organizations, and business and professional associations for everyone from car dealers to doctors. In most communities the list is a long one, and every one of those organizations has meetings. Get on the phone (starting with friends and acquaintances, where possible) and see if you can't get on the agenda for at least one of those functions every month. The topic? Flying, of course!

Start or Support Local Aviation Clubs

As a flight instructor, you hold the key to fostering public interest in aviation. One very effective way to do that is to organize interest groups for people interested in flying. One instructor I know started an aviation club for high school students. He contacted high schools in his metropolitan area, identified which faculty members might be supportive, met with them, and then organized a free club to meet monthly at his flight school.

Attendance was excellent from the first meeting on. The instructor arranged tours of airport facilities, and speakers from different aviation professions. Of course, he was immediately deluged with requests by students for introductory flights (he quickly arranged a package deal with his flight school). A number of young club members immediately went on to take flying lessons.

Similar support can tie in nicely with community college or university aviation clubs, and with other local organizations. Work with Boy Scouts of America to set up an Aviation Explorer post; start by applying to the district scout council as an aviation merit badge counselor. For the same reasons consider joining or hosting activities for local Civil Air Patrol squadrons.

Advertise

You may think that advertising is too expensive for your budget, but it's not, if you're clever about it. The trick is to go for broad coverage, rather than glamour, and to watch for cost-effective opportunities to advertise to likely audiences.

Newspaper Classifieds

Many CFIs run ads in local newspapers, which is certainly a good place to start. Two types of advertisements are available to you in the paper: "Classifieds" are the "want ads" where you sold your unicycle last year. "Display ads" are the larger commercial ads which often include logos and pictures.

Repetition is one of the keys to success in advertising, so don't let the newspaper advertising department talk you into a fancy display ad you can afford to insert only a few times. The odds are slim that many prospective students will notice a one-time ad, and even those who do may need to see it for months before responding to it.

It's always better to insert a smaller ad you can afford to run indefinitely. Flying is not heavily advertised in most newspapers, anyway, so if someone is interested in flying lessons, you've got a good shot at them with a care-fully-written classified listed under "Aircraft," or "Aviation." Over time with many insertions, more people will see your ad regularly, and recognize you as an established business. When the time comes to start flying, they'll look for "that flight instruction ad I always see in the Sunday paper."

"Even the classifieds get expensive," you may be thinking, "if you run them every day." True, but who thinks of flying lessons on a Monday morning? Place your ads to run only on weekends or Sundays.

Gift Certificates and Learn-to-Fly Packages
Incidentally, if you do want to try some higher-profile one-time display ads, consider offering gift certificates, perhaps tied to an upcoming holiday. Gift certificates are more like products than services, since the purchaser pays a one-time price and gets a single usable item in return. They are easier to sell as an impulse buy than a course of flying lessons, and are therefore better suited to one-time advertising. "Introductory flying lesson" certificates make nice gifts, require little expertise to sell, and get you up in the air with a person who someone thought would enjoy flying.

Incidentally, one flight school I know has taken the gift certificate concept a step further and developed a classy learn-to-fly gift package. Each beauti-fully wrapped box includes a logbook, private pilot textbook, and a certifi-cate valued at one hour of aircraft rental plus 1.4 hours of flight instruction. Also included is a polo shirt embroidered with the flight school logo.

Organization Newsletters and Bulletin Boards
Take advantage of your connections. Advertising in organization newslet-ters is inexpensive or free, plus you have the added advantage of another common interest with the readers. Run ads in your homeowner's associa-tion, church and charity newsletters, and post fliers on their bulletin boards.

It's also wise to target the kinds of local executives and professionals whom you know can afford lessons. Go to your local Chamber of Commerce, and find out about regional business and professional societies and service organizations. Along with the Chamber of Commerce member newsletter, look for advertising opportunities with the county medical and dental societies, and within comparable organizations of attorneys, accountants and business people.

Telephone Book Ads

If you're in the instructing business to stay, an ad in the phone book is very important. In fact, many FBOs say that the "yellow pages" are their single largest source of inquiries. It's important to note, however, that the percentage of *qualified* inquiries from the phone book often tends to be a bit lower than from other sources.

Phone book advertising requires leasing of a business telephone line, and is not inexpensive. The lead time required to place such an ad can run up to a year or more, and carries with it an additional one or two year commitment to pay for it.

For these reasons, it's well worth your while to call companies who already advertise there, and quiz them about their success with various ad sizes and designs. Also, most telephone companies offer excellent guidance on developing an ad appropriate to your budget and business. Be sure to seek out an experienced advertising representative when designing and placing your ad.

Direct Mail

The term "direct mail" refers to the process of sending large numbers of fliers to prospective customers by mail. It's a tough thing to do well, and can be expensive.

Let's say you borrow Mom's life savings from the cookie jar, print a fabulous "Learn to Fly with Norman" brochure, and mail it away to 500 listings from the phone book. Sales and marketing experts expect a one percent response rate from most direct mail campaigns, so five replies of any kind (including wrong numbers), would be a reasonable return. Unless there's lots more money in that cookie jar, you may be sorely disappointed.

It's easy to see why it takes a large organization to make money on direct mail: huge mailing lists are often necessary to provide the right balance of responses with economy of scale in printing and mailing.

For small operators, direct mail does have its role, but rarely as a stand-alone method to build business. For our purposes, mailings are best used as part of a broader program to inform existing clients of special offerings, and to keep your name alive among prospective students.

Broadcast Media

Finally, don't categorically rule out advertising on TV and radio before checking all the options. The costs in smaller communities and on public access channels can be surprisingly reasonable.

One particularly affordable way to promote your business on radio is to sponsor a program on your local National Public Radio station. For only a few dollars a week you can get your name and a one-line flying message out to the public on a regular basis. And, like volunteer work your support for public radio gives something back to your local community.

PUTTING IT ALL TOGETHER

Obviously not everyone will do everything that was discussed in the last few pages at once—this has been a lot of ground to cover. On the other hand, the more broadly you promote your flight instruction services, the happier you'll be with the results.

In order to make sense out of all this, the next step is for you to research the options we've discussed. Visit the chamber of commerce and learn about local organizations and activities. Check on advertising rates, and current aviation offerings in the community. Who's offering flight-related seminars and ground schools, and on what topics?

If possible, meet with some of those local service professionals discussed here—attorneys, dentists and insurance people. Learn which organizations and methods they've found most productive locally. Talk to your flight school, if you currently work with one, about what level of support they might be willing to provide for your promotional efforts. All of this can be done in only a few days of concentrated effort, and will help tremendously in putting a plan together. But a question naturally arises from this chapter's discussion: "As I meet all of those prospective flight students, what do I do with them?"

FOUR

Converting Prospects Into Flight Students

Last chapter we talked a good deal about how and where to meet prospective flight students. The next question is how to "close" those prospects — convert them from "wannabe" pilots to flight students. There are several factors in the process of closing students. First is to determine whether people you meet are truly interested. The second has to do with keeping your better prospects hot over time, if they're not quite ready to sign up on the day you meet them. Finally, there's the need to provide the support and encouragement which motivates them to take the big step.

How Do You Know When You've Met a Serious Prospect?

So you're out there shaking the bushes for your next flight student. How can you tell which of the people you meet are serious prospects for your instructing services? Before you invest too much time trying to sell someone on lessons, there are a few key indicators to consider.

Theoretically, any number of people you meet will be interested in taking flying lessons. The problem instructors run up against is that many prospects are only casually interested. As a result, it's all too easy to invest time and energy into pursuing a prospective student, only to find out the person is not likely to take the plunge during this lifetime.

So like salespeople in any field, you've got to learn how to identify and separate the serious customers worth pursuing, from those who don't want to tell you they're not interested for fear of hurting your feelings. Sales pros call these serious customers "qualified prospects." How does one identify them? Well, it's definitely more like a "sixth sense" than a science, but most sales types would agree that qualified prospects have the desire, the need, and the money to buy. For our purposes in attracting new flight students, qualified prospects are people who want to become pilots, have the money to take lessons, and are ready to start flying. Ready, willing, and able, you might say.

Anybody not meeting all three of these criteria on a given day is not going to start lessons. In fact, for any person not meeting two of the three criteria, it's pretty safe to assume without further consideration that this person is not going to take flying lessons anytime soon, and it is best to move on to someone new.

Can They Afford to Take Lessons?

No matter how much someone wants to become a pilot, if they don't have the money it's not going to happen. No amount of wishing is going to pay for flying lessons. What's more, you're performing no service by taking on a student who can't afford to do it right; the thoughts of an impoverished student are on how to pay the bill for today's lesson, not on how to fly the airplane.

It's also difficult for you as instructor to avoid getting dragged into such a student's financial concerns. First thing you know, you're skipping the session that "sure would help" on crosswind landings because the student can't afford any extra flights. It's better for everyone concerned if students wait to take lessons until they can properly afford it.

How Strong is Their Desire to Fly?

Occasionally you'll meet someone who has the money to take lessons and is sort of shopping around, but doesn't really have that big-time desire to fly. (You know the type: walks right past the P-51 on the ramp, without noticing it.)

People like this are usually image-conscious individuals who think it would be neat to tell others that they're pilots, but who are either frightened, uninterested in the details of flying, or unwilling to do the work. They'll talk to you a lot and perhaps take a lesson or two, but the genuine interest isn't there. No "fire" in their eyes. Along with being poor prospects, tire kickers like these are capable of consuming many unproductive hours talking to you, until they can come up with a face-saving excuse not to do the lessons.

I once met a financially successful fellow who claimed to love flying. He could discuss the design and performance of many different aircraft models, and had actually taken some lessons in the past. But after weeks of casual discussion, nothing had come of all that indicated interest. I just couldn't figure out why someone so apparently enthusiastic hadn't gotten back into flying.

Finally, after lots of hangar flying, the truth came out. He had learned that his life insurance premiums might go up if he became a pilot. Therefore, he told me, he had decided to quit the lessons and put off learning to fly for ten or fifteen years, until he'd paid off his whole life insurance policy. How badly could this guy want to fly?!

Are They Ready to Start?

Now for the third indicator of a qualified prospect: how urgently does the person need or want to start lessons?

Yes, it's obviously best to meet someone who wants to start flying tomorrow, but don't give up on the folks who are seriously interested but just a little hesitant. If someone really wants to take flying lessons and can easily afford to do it, you've got a darned good shot at them. Even if "not quite ready" today, that person could become your student reasonably soon, next week or in a month or two.

Think of it this way. Why would someone who really wants to fly and who has the money, not take flying lessons? Probably hasn't met the right instructor yet!

Actually, there's another reason why people who would love to fly sometimes haven't pursued it. The give-away comes when someone you meet learns that you are a pilot. That wild, glazed look, with which all pilots (and their spouses) are familiar, appears in the victim's eyes, and stories begin tumbling out about long-ago airplane rides with an uncle who once flew DC-3s for Pan Am.

These are people with misperceptions about what it takes to become a pilot. It's fun meeting them, because you don't have to sell them on flying; they already love it even more than you do! What's more, they think that a Cessna 152 is a neat airplane, and are impressed that you fly one. But for some reason, these folks' own dream of flying has remained unfulfilled. Sometimes there's a good reason they never learned to fly themselves, such as a health problem. But in many cases they've never taken lessons for some not-so-good reason; for example, thinking that they were too old, or that you can't be a pilot if you wear glasses.

Closet aviators like these aren't necessarily easy to win over, because they've disqualified themselves emotionally long ago. Many of them will learn to fly only if they connect with an instructor under just the right circumstances—being introduced by a friend, or getting to know one under casual circumstances. For these folks meeting the right instructor brings a kind of subliminal interest to the surface. If you are the one who can re-awaken the interest and get them started on flying, you'll share their joy in fulfilling a life-long dream.

ADDRESSING YOUR PROSPECTS' CONCERNS — AND THEIR FAMILIES'

The concerns of prospective pilots are generally predictable, so it's worth the time to consider what they are, and how you and your flight school might best deal with them. By getting the concerns of your prospects out in the open, you at least have the opportunity to perhaps allay some of their fears. And even if some of your prospect's concerns are never actually stated out loud, at least you can try to cover some likely ones in your answers to their questions. Remember that in most cases, you'll have to address not only the personal concerns expressed by the potential student, but also the apprehensions of a family behind the scenes.

How Much Does It Cost To Fly?

This is one of the toughest questions a prospective flight student can ask, because the answer is potentially so complicated. The simple and obvious answer is a flat number for Private Pilot training, like "$3,500." Over time, however, one learns that spouting that sort of quick answer often doesn't work very well, primarily because everyone's frame of reference is so different when it comes to money. Flight instructors must be particularly careful in this regard because they almost always earn much less than their students. (Probably a red placard should be mounted on the door from every instructors' lounge to the reception area, stating, *"Warning! Do Not Equate Your Personal Financial Status with that of Your Student!"*)

Keep in mind that with most prospective customers, their biggest concern is not the total amount of money they need to invest, but rather it is whether they'll get "ripped off." In other words, most are perfectly prepared to pay a fair price for flight training; they just want to make sure they're getting a fair deal.

Another factor in this cost issue is cash flow. People these days are well-accustomed to making purchases in the price range of flying lessons, but it's usually done in a manner which spreads out the payments. So another approach is to tell prospects, "The most cost-effective way to take lessons is with a minimum of two sessions per week, so you'll retain what you learn from one lesson to the next. Based on an investment of seventy-five to eighty dollars per lesson, that should give you a good idea of what to budget each week."

Even customers who can easily write a check for four or five thousand dollars often prefer to make sure they like what they're getting for it, before signing on the dotted line. Accordingly, "pay as you go" is very attractive to many flight training customers, not only because it spreads out the investment into manageable chunks, but also because they feel more control of the investment and the decision to continue.

Another critical thing to understand is that *many people who think they can't afford flying are not concerned about the cost of the lessons.* That may sound strange, but it comes back to more of those widely-held misconceptions about being a pilot. Many prospects have gathered through the grapevine that pilots must continually practice and retrain to maintain their skills. This of course is perfectly true, and is in fact the mark of a good pilot. But prospects often think that the cost and time investments required to stay current are orders of magnitude greater than they really are. Be prepared to briefly discuss currency requirements for private pilots; as we all know, staying proficient, especially for VFR (visual flight rules) flying, is not very expensive.

People often think flying will be prohibitively expensive even when the lessons are over, perhaps because they see aircraft rental rates posted at $50, $60, and even $100 per hour. You simply cannot address the cost of flying without giving some examples of what a great deal flying is *after* they've earned their certificate!

"Yes, Mr. Simpson, a four-seat airplane does rent for $65 per hour. Let's consider for a moment what an incredible deal that really is. You mentioned earlier that you and your wife often drive up to Burlington. Let's say that after earning your private pilot certificate, the two of you decide to fly up there for the day with another couple. That's about two hundred road miles away.

"Since our Cessna 172 cruises at around 135 statute miles per hour, the four of you can be at Burlington in an hour and a half, versus four hours each way driving windy roads in your car. Since you pay plane rental only for time while the engine is running, and the hourly rate includes fuel, the total round-trip cost per person to fly there works out to under $50. Not only will everyone still be fresh when they get to Burlington, but you won't need to pay for a hotel room and take an extra day off, as you do when you drive there!"

The point is that when your prospective students start asking about the cost of lessons, be sure to tell them the *whole* story. Ask them about some places they like to go, and show them what an incredible value flying really is.

Now back to the bottom line. Yes, we do indeed need to tell prospects what they should expect to invest to earn a private pilot certificate. Just remember that people are more concerned about being treated fairly than about getting the lowest price; so when the time comes to detail training costs, the worst thing you can do is "lowball" the investment required. When your car needs repair, nothing is more upsetting than being underquoted up front, and having to foot a larger-than-expected bill when it's over. Yet severe underquoting is typical in our industry.

Be totally honest about what it's going to cost: "You'll notice from our private pilot information sheet that it's technically possible to earn a pilot certificate in thirty-five hours, but that's simply not realistic for most people. Based on our experience here at the flight school, I recommend budgeting around $4,000 to $4,500 to earn your private pilot certificate."

Offering a range in this way is valuable because it gives you the chance to show how the customer can impact his or her own investment. "We find that a great deal of the training investment boils down to the motivation and availability of the individual student. Of course there can be factors outside of our control, like weather. But if you prepare well and are able fly regularly, it may well be possible achieve to the lower end of that range."

Why am I so sure they'll listen to you? Because you're the expert, of course, and you're being frank with them. When you share the straight facts about their upcoming investment, prospects feel much more comfortable about proceeding.

If you've done a good job of explaining the benefits of being a pilot, and are honest with them, most customers will find the true cost of admission very reasonable. And they'll be a lot more likely to finish the certificate if the costs along the way pan out close to what you've told them to expect.

Am I Too Old to Become a Pilot?

This question and the next one about wearing glasses are probably the two most common concerns which prevent people from becoming aviators. Those of us who already fly know that many pilots remain active into their seventies, eighties and occasionally beyond.

But for some reason, perhaps relating to the popularity of fighter pilot novels and movies, many people labor under the misconception that if they're older than thirty or thirty-five, they do not possess the hair-trigger reflexes required to pilot a Warrior around the pattern!

No kidding, I receive inquiries almost every day with questions like, "I'm 44 and have finally reached the point in life where I can afford to learn to fly. But I've always been told that flying is a young person's skill. Am I too old to learn?"

The best arguments for selling such folks are examples; tell them about older pilots you have personally trained. Then arrange for them to call or meet some older pilots, preferably including someone who has recently earned a pilot certificate. For prospects in their forties or fifties who express concern about age, explain that airline pilots routinely fly giant airliners all over the globe, up to age sixty.

Finally, for those prospects really hung up on the youthful reflexes thing, I like to point out the relative importance of good judgment, which tends to develop with age, as compared to physical responses when piloting an airplane. If you think about it, hair-trigger reflexes are rarely required in civilian flying; when they do become necessary it's usually because an earlier lapse in judgment has unnecessarily put the aircraft into a tight situation.

To illustrate, I tell the story of an incident that occurred a number of years ago in the midwest involving a King Air. The young pilot had departed IFR (instrument flight rules) for a short flight of only eighty miles, when about halfway to his destination, both engines flamed out simultaneously. The aircraft descended in the soup down to four or five hundred feet above ground, having the good fortune to break out directly over a nearly-deserted stretch of freeway.

This fellow masterfully landed his stricken turboprop dead-stick on the freeway without harm to himself, the vehicle or anyone else. On the following day, the local newspaper made a big deal about the miraculous skill of this pilot, in safely landing with no engine power, "after his plane ran out of fuel." Needless to say those of us at the airport were not so impressed. Here's a case where the need for youthful reflexes could have been elegantly avoided, using even the tiniest dose of good judgment about fuel reserves.

Of course, as with any other prospect, one of the best ways to deal with concerns about age is to schedule an introductory flight lesson. (More on that in the next chapter.)

But I Wear Glasses...
The other question which simply will not go away has to do with vision requirements for pilots. "I wear glasses, so I can't be a pilot, right?" We should all shudder to think of the number of aviation enthusiasts who have always wanted to be pilots, but never took lessons because they thought wearing glasses disqualified them.

In keeping with your role as a resource and an expert, make it your business to know, at least in general terms, the current medical requirements as they pertain to pilots wearing glasses.

Is it Safe?
Many instructors like to keep the latest safety statistics at hand, so they can be shared with prospects who express that particular concern about flying. But I have found a more intuitive approach to be effective. When a prospect brings up the safety issue, I simply ask the question, "What's the one thing about driving that scares you most?" It may take a moment's thought, but the answer can be predicted almost without fail. "That somebody going the other way will cross the centerline, just as I come over a hill," says your prospect, or "that some jerk will pull out in front of me when I least expect it."

Flying largely eliminates the greatest fear of drivers: the fear of "the other guy." After pointing out that mid-air collisions are very rare, I emphasize that the largest percentage of accidents can be avoided through due diligence and good judgment. In short, with flying you are almost totally in control of your own destiny. Pilots who properly plan their trips, ensure there's enough fuel in the plane to get to their destinations, don't do stunts close to the ground, and avoid known bad weather, can anticipate the likelihood of a lasting, enjoyable, and safe experience.

I then take time to reinforce the "known" in "known bad weather." It's really pretty rare in aviation that pilots experience accidents due to the unknown (or else we'd all quit flying); rather, flying safely is more often an issue of avoiding known risks. Most people interested in flying are confident in their own skills; when they feel that they will control their own safety, they usually feel pretty good about it.

Family Fears

Who is it you're selling when a prospect comes to the airport? The prospective pilot, of course. But not so obvious are the people behind the scenes who must also be convinced that becoming a pilot is such a great idea. In many cases you'll need to provide the support your prospect needs to sell his or her family on the idea that flying is safe, affordable, a good financial investment, and something that the prospect is capable of doing.

Now here's the funny part. We in aviation have become accustomed to selling flying based on cost-justification, practicality, and safety. The average prospect, however, wants to be convinced, at least emotionally, that flying will be adventurous and fun. Does that mean we should stop promoting the practical aspects of flying? No way. Those practical and safety aspects are what the prospect needs to sell the folks back home. Keep that in mind when designing your next brochure. Sell the prospect on adventure, then have him or her carry home a brochure that demonstrates the safety and practicality of general aviation.

Keeping Them Hot When They're Not Ready to Start

Instructors are an impatient bunch. After all, many of us are trying to build flight experience as quickly as possible, so anyone who doesn't want to start flying right now isn't of much interest to us. But this is a very shortsighted attitude.

Sure, it's great meeting someone who's ready to start flying "right now." But the odds are slim for meeting a great number of prospects at precisely the moment when they have all three of those qualifiers—the money, the desire, and the time to begin flying lessons.

More likely, on the day you meet a prospective student, there's some reason why "today" is not ideal for starting. It may be a new baby, personal problems, financial or business commitments—any number of darned good reasons. What must be kept in mind is that people's situations can suddenly change. Although now may not be the appropriate time for starting flight training, a few short weeks in the future could be.

Realize that closet aviators can sometimes sit on piloting plans for years. Then one day something happens, and suddenly a student is ready to start "tomorrow." It could be a large tax refund, a raise or promotion, or the fact that a son or daughter has finished college. For many people, flying lessons are a response to the middle-age blues—time to learn something new and exciting.

The point of all this is that since it's so tough to meet every prospect on the day he or she is ready to start, you need to keep your name alive so you'll get the call when the urge does strike. How do you set yourself up to get the call on the day your prospect is ready?

Let's say you're working out at the health club, when another member spots your "flying inverted" T-shirt. He comes over and begins chatting with you, asking all sorts of good questions about taking flying lessons. It quickly becomes apparent that you've met a particularly enthusiastic and friendly pilot "wannabe." Better yet, the guy consents to meet you at the airport the next day and have a look around.

At your meeting the following day the two of you hit it off right away. The prospective pilot is a nice guy, sharp, and friendly. He appears to have the right combination of judgment and enthusiasm, and expresses high personal interest and good business reasons for becoming a pilot. What's more, he's already talking about earning his instrument and multi-engine ratings after his private pilot certificate. The two of you have some interests in common, and it's obvious that you've made a great impression. In short, this fellow would make a great student.

After an enjoyable introductory lesson, and a otherwise pleasant meeting all around, your health club buddy heads for the door. "You seem like a well-qualified instructor," he says, "and the type of individual I'd enjoy working with. Unfortunately, this is a poor time for me to start flying lessons, as I'm in the midst of a major project for my company requiring lots of travel. I could be saddled with it for months! Thanks for showing me around, and good luck."

Consider this: if that prospective student suddenly finds the time to start lessons tomorrow, will he call you? Sure. Will you be remembered after a week? Probably. After a month? It's possible, but less likely. Ninety days?

Let's face it, the longer it is between the day of your meeting and when the student finds himself ready, the less likely that he'll remember you, or for that matter, that he'll pursue flying lessons at all.

The odds of catching such a prospect on exactly the right day are slim, but if you can maintain a presence and a positive impression for a month, your odds improve. Is the student someone you or your flight school would be interested in after six months or a year?

The point is to keep your name alive in the heads of your best prospects for a good while after the first meeting. That way when the urge and the opportunity do strike, you'll find yourself in a great position to gain a new flight student.

Set Up a Filing System
Keeping your name alive with your prospects requires setting up a simple filing system. This may be done in any number of ways, from files in a file drawer to index cards in a recipe box. If you have access to a personal computer with database or personal information software installed, that's even better.

Each time you meet someone new, create a new file and make a few notes about that person's situation, business, and any specific interests he or she may have. This is important, because if you're communicating with more than three or four prospects at a time, you'll forget a lot about them individually if you don't keep notes.

Next, organize your leads so that you'll be sure to contact everyone on a regular basis. Again, this can be done with many computer software programs, or it can be as simple as posting a list at your desk showing each of your flight training prospects, along with a check-off column for each month. Determine ahead of time how often to be in contact with each person on your list, and then check off the tracking sheet accordingly.

Make it your goal to touch base with each of your prospective flight students at least once per month. Any less often that that, and those folks are much less likely to impulsively phone you if the opportunity arises to start lessons.

Keeping In Touch By Mail

Once a month may seem like a lot; most of us are appropriately sensitive about calling someone very often and asking, "Are you ready to start flying lessons yet?" There are, however, some effective, low-key ways to casually keep in touch with your prospects on a regular basis without pestering anybody. Note that most of these take very little time to execute.

Holiday Cards

You can't go wrong with holiday cards. People are always glad to receive cards on special occasions, and take them only in the spirit of the season. Obviously, the most appropriate cards for these purposes convey holiday wishes in the context of an aviation theme. Just be sensitive to avoid any religious connotations unless you really know the person. Be sure that your cards are tasteful, since everyone's sense of humor is different.

Magazine Articles

Another good vehicle for keeping in touch is the magazine article. Anytime you read something that might interest one or more of your prospects, make some copies. Directly on the article (so your name will be saved with it), jot down a friendly note: "Hi Bill, thought you'd find this interesting!" Sign it with your full name, attach your business card (if appropriate), mail it away, and check off your tracking sheet for the month.

Ideally, articles you choose should directly relate to the specific flying interests that each prospective student told you about. A not-too-technical aerobatics article, for example, would be appropriate for prospects who've expressed interest in flying they saw at airshows. Articles about flying trips to out-of-the way destinations are ideal for those interested in travel. And how about a fly-in fishing article for the outdoor types?

Hunting for articles may sound like too much work, but it's not. Just keep your eyes open for interesting features in the course of your normal reading. (I hate to admit how many magazine pages I've snatched from the doctor's office waiting room.) Certain "popular" publications are great for offbeat aviation-related articles. *Smithsonian Air & Space*, for example, runs articles on a wide variety of aviation topics, each presented in an interesting and non-technical manner.

Articles are great promotional tools because they show that you know a little about your friends' interests, which everyone finds complimentary. You're certainly asking for nothing when you send such material. At worst, the recipient will just think "nice thought," note your name, and throw the article away. At best, you'll brighten someone's day with something that may entice them out to the airport to get started on those lessons.

Postcards and Greeting Cards

Postcards and greeting cards are terrific for keeping in casual contact. Writing them takes very little time, and postcards even save on postage costs. But here's the kicker: have you ever received a postcard you didn't read?

Be on the lookout for interesting postcards and greeting cards relating to flying, and when you find some, buy a supply for future use. Postcards depicting exotic airports and interesting aircraft always catch people's eyes, as do cards featuring appropriate humor.

Newsletters

Newsletters are fairly popular for use as promotional tools in the flight training business, but one has to be both focused and careful in using them. Sure, you can cover a training topic or two in each issue, as long as the articles are brief.

But the emphasis should be on stories about flying trips, reviews of exciting flight destinations, and profiles of student pilots and pilots at your flight school. The main focus of a promotional newsletter should be to show prospects all the fun they'll have when they become pilots, showcasing activities at the flight school in the process.

Remember that if you're going to do newsletters they must be produced monthly, like clockwork, and they should be broad enough to appeal to both prospective pilots and current flight school customers, thus aiding in both attracting new students and keeping the current ones interested. New prospective pilots you meet should go on the mailing list for six to twelve months—call them every two to three months to ask if they'd still like to receive it, and to invite them out to the airport. Current students and customers should receive the newsletter indefinitely.

Getting Attention With Your Mail

Just about every one of us looks forward to opening our mail, until we find out that there's nothing in it but bills! That's why it's so important to make your written communications look personal and interesting, even before they're opened. For communicating with your prospects, buy aviation-related stamps when available. When they're not, use something else bright and colorful for postage. Even the selection of an interesting stamp is a personal touch not found on most mail. (Do not use a postage machine for any personal communications!)

It's also easy (and fun for the recipient) to personalize your notes and letters in other ways. Consider having a rubber stamp made of your favorite airplane, to apply on envelopes. (Custom rubber stamps can be ordered at many quick-print shops; just bring in a picture or drawing of your favorite airplane.) One fellow I know sends packages to his contacts wrapped in obsolete aeronautical charts. You can bet that his mail gets opened promptly!

Again, each prospect should experience some sort of contact with you or your organization at least once per month. It doesn't matter so much how that contact is made, just that it happens. Don't be misled by the number of alternatives we've just covered for staying in touch by mail. If your prospect receives the same postcard every month for three months in a row, that's perfectly okay. It's not variety you're looking for, but rather a presence. (In fact, most companies tend to grow tired of their marketing materials long before their customers do.) Just be sure your prospects hear from you somehow at least once a month, every month.

Personal Contact

Phone calls and meetings are a little tougher to inject into the process. It's important to talk with your prospective flight students periodically in order to keep the human connection alive. On the other hand, many of your best prospects are probably busy people, if they're worth staying in touch with.

Try to telephone or make an appointment to meet at least every few months. Have a specific purpose in mind when you phone, like to invite prospects to an event at the flight school, to renew the newsletter subscription, or to advise them of an upcoming special. (More than an occasional "How're you doing?" call makes you a pest.)

Telephone calls should always open with the question (after identifying yourself), "Is this a good time to call?" If it is not, "When is a good time to call back?" Note the answer and follow up accordingly.

One excellent approach is to host gatherings for flight students and prospects every month or two. That allows you several contacts with prospective customers: a written invitation, a follow-up telephone call to personally invite them out to the airport, the meeting itself, and a "thanks for coming" card. And the announcements for these sorts of gatherings can usually be run at no charge in the "community news and events" section of the local paper, providing you fax over a news release well in advance.

TAKE PROSPECTS FLYING

There's no better way to interest prospective pilots than to — you've guessed it — take them flying. Just remember that the flight needs to be a great experience, or you might never get another opportunity.

When you're doing some pleasure flying, or instructing a student in a four-place airplane, invite a prospect (or have your student invite one) to join you. Needless to say, pick a smooth day weather-wise and a mission that will be enjoyable. Stalls and steep turns won't sell many new students on flying.

In many cases, it's best to set up a short pleasure trip for qualified prospective students. (Remember that "qualified" means having the money and the desire!) Consider a Saturday morning flight to an interesting place for breakfast. Stick with straight and level flying, and keep each leg to an hour or less. You'll be asked many questions throughout the trip, and the opportunity will arise to talk about lessons. In many cases, if the trip is pleasant your prospect will be ready to schedule the first lesson upon landing.

Sharing the Adventure:
That All-Important Introductory Lesson

Here it is—your best opportunity to sell a new student on flying! By the time someone has actually made an appointment for an introductory lesson, and gone to the trouble of driving to the airport, we know that he or she is pretty enthused about flying before ever arriving. Our mission appears simple enough; translate that enthusiasm into action.

If the prospect has a good time and feels confident in his or her ability to learn to fly, you've probably won yourself a student. But if major questions are raised in the prospective student's mind, like "I'm not sure I can do this," "I don't like this outfit," "Is flying safe?" or "This isn't cool," you're probably out of luck.

In short, the introductory lesson offers a great opportunity to make—or break—the sale.

ANATOMY OF A "TYPICAL" INTRO FLIGHT

Everyone knows about "intro flights," right? The customer walks in the door and presents a coupon at the front desk of the flight school. Some instructor who's not busy takes the visitor up for a twenty-minute plane ride, just to show them what flying is all about. The manager has already cautioned the instructing staff to keep such flights brief, because there's no money in intro flights, which is fine because everybody at the office is pretty busy hangar-flying, anyway.

After the flight is over, the instructor quickly walks the prospect back out to the front counter (already running late for the next lesson), and says something like, "Well, hope you enjoyed it. Give us a call if you decide you want to take lessons." The CFI then runs back out the door to the ramp.

How'd we do? Was it a great experience? Will the prospect be back? In answer let's consider the impressions of one very typical aspiring pilot after completing his intro flight.

"Dear Greg,

I just got back from my demonstration ride and I have mixed feelings. I did find the ride exhilarating, but very overwhelming (it's my first flight in a small plane). The Cessna 152 seemed to need constant correction for level flight. I would have thought that with the aircraft properly trimmed very little pilot input would have been necessary. I also had trouble with the rudder. Incidentally I'm the kind of person who doesn't care to ride in cars with other people driving. Do you find these feelings common in other students?

Secondly, I'm not sure about the ethics of the flight school I've been considering. When I first went to the flight school I was given a card outlining the Part 141 training cost. I told them I needed a more detailed summary to submit to my employer for payment re-imbursement. I was then given a handwritten note on company letterhead outlining the Part 141 cost and it was $200 higher. The ground and flight training times were the same on both quotes. In fact, I can't find anything on the note that isn't on the card. When I asked about the difference I was given some mumbo jumbo about the card not listing all the supplies. Ok, Ok, I'm easy; I just accepted it. My employer was going to pay for at least part of it anyway.

I asked about a demonstration flight and scheduled one. After the demonstration flight I was presented a bill for $60. I was shocked, I'm 43 and I've never had to pay for any kind of demonstration before in my life. I figured the demonstration flight would be free just to sell me on their school. Guess not, at least not in this industry. Or is it? Would you feel comfortable with this school?"

"Tom"

Not a very fulfilling conclusion to all that work we just invested in getting that prospect out to the airport, is it? The fact is that many of us love flying so much, it's hard to imagine someone *not* dying to sign up after the intro flight. But only diehard enthusiasts like ourselves will call back next week and schedule a lesson, after an intro flight as we've just described it.

From the flight school perspective, it would be easy enough to rationalize this customer away. No one can expect to master flying an airplane in one lesson. We all know the difficulty of nailing down the exact cost of earning a private pilot certificate. And virtually every flight school charges for intro flights. If Tom can't afford to spend $60 for an intro flight, how can we expect him to come up with the cash to complete the training?

But Tom found the flight "exhilarating." He appears to be the type of thoughtful and intelligent individual who would make a good pilot. And the tone of his letter suggests that he wanted to be sold on flying, and is disappointed that he wasn't. Do we really want to lose him? Perhaps a perfectly good flight student just got away.

What, in Tom's case, could have been done to leave him with a better impression? First, Tom's intro ride was probably either too short or too detailed, leaving him with doubts about mastering the required skills. Since it is our most important sales tool, every intro lesson *must* be a terrific experience for our customers. We must begin each one having a specific plan of what we are going to do, and end it with an analysis of how the experience can be improved for the next customer. Did the instructor tell Tom he did a good job? And was he formally invited to schedule the next lesson?

As for the training costs, clearly it would have helped if they had been summarized *in print*—with some discussion about how they were derived—so Tom would feel more comfortable about signing on the dotted line. Note that he did not take issue with the prices, only with the lack of consistency.

However, when I telephoned Tom in response to his letter, I learned that the problem was deeper than even he realized. The flight training estimates he refers to were $2,600 and $2,800 respectively, figures based on 35-hour Part 141 training minimums. Obviously those are totally unrealistic for a once- or twice-a-week pleasure flying student. Do you think Tom would have been happy, halfway through training, when he began running over budget? Yet how many flight schools deliver these sorts of estimates? As we discussed last chapter, many CFIs and flight schools do not feel confident about presenting the real costs to their customers, for fear of driving them away.

When I suggested to Tom that he budget around $4,000 for flight training, and explained the factors affecting that figure, he wasn't phased a bit. In fact he was perfectly satisfied. Knowing how the investment was arrived at, and how he could impact it, made him perfectly comfortable to proceed with training.

Then there's the intro flight. While it's true that most flight schools charge for them, Tom's observation that most other demonstrations are free is true. It didn't help that nobody told him he'd have to pay for it until it was over! No wonder he was angry. Yet once I assured him that paying for the intro flight is normal in our industry, he was entirely comfortable with the $60 investment.

Now for the really important question. Which of these complaints caused us to almost lose Tom as a flight student? Probably no one of them alone, though they had the cumulative effect of adding doubts. Tom went to the airport seeking something much deeper than these problems he wrote about would suggest: perhaps his word, "exhilaration" offers us a clue as to what he was really looking for. To make his dream come true he was prepared to invest whatever money, and overcome whatever obstacles it took to become a pilot. How do I know this is true? Because after five minutes of telephone "damage control," Tom was back to planning his flying lessons.

What, then, constitutes a great experience? And what can we do to meet the expectations of each prospective customer?

To properly address this issue, let's back up a few steps and consider some of the forces at work in the minds of our prospects when they decide to come out for the intro flight.

YOUR PROSPECTS WANT TO BE PILOTS, NOT STUDENTS!

The single most important thing to realize about your prospects is that *every one of them wants to be a pilot, not a student!* Let's climb inside their minds for a moment, and imagine the videos playing there during the drive to the airport. Here are a few likely scenes:

- Stepping out of a sleek and sexy airplane, ten pounds thinner and accompanied by an attractive companion.

- Friends and family experiencing a perfect landing alongside a beautiful beach, their faces filled with admiration.

- Awestruck business associates, impressed by a Tom Cruise look-alike stepping from the pilot seat of his Learjet.

- Dashing woman pilot unloading skis from her personal airplane at Vail, her hair blowing stylishly in the breeze.

- And of course, being summoned to the "front office" of an airliner to save the day by landing the plane, both airline pilots having become incapacitated.

Ridiculous? Absolutely not! People become pilots because flying is exciting and challenging, because the view from above is spectacular, and because others will admire them for their accomplishment.

But for some reason, often around the time we start instructing, many of us in flight training tend to forget the glamour and the excitement that brought us into aviation. Maybe part of the problem is a tendency for professional pilots to mask their love of flying, to "look professional," as it were. But we must never forget that our job as instructors is to foster enthusiasm in our students, not kill it. And that attitude must start with each and every new student, on the occasion of the introductory lesson.

Just to reinforce the point, let's consider for a moment some movies which definitely are *not* playing in the heads of those "wannabe" pilots, on that drive to the airport:

- Sitting in ground school attentively taking notes.

- Trying to wash the fuel-smell off their hands and the oil stain off their sleeves, before going to work.

- Savoring the art of mastering power-on stalls, from the cramped 120-degree cockpit of a Tomahawk.

- Scraping ice off the top of a Cessna wing in sub-zero temperatures.

- Driving home in the rain after the fourth "today-was-supposed-to-be-solo" lesson canceled by bad weather.

- Gleefully learning crosswind landings on a twenty-foot-wide runway while the instructor grips the dash for dear life.

Folks, your students are going to learn the realities of flight training plenty soon enough. Earning a private pilot's certificate is a lot of work, and not everyone has what it takes to do it. But the biggest reason for anyone to see it all the way through is *the reward of being a pilot, when it's over*.

Everyone wants to be a pilot: confident, suave, accomplished. Nobody wants to be a student: fawning, timid, discouraged. If you can keep that distinction in mind from the first contact with each prospective new student, through the very last day of ATP training, you'll sign up plenty of new students and lose very few along the way. But the day your students feel like *students*, the first doubts will arise in their minds. And if that feeling continues for more than a few lessons in a row, you've lost them.

If it seems I'm making a big deal out of this first introductory flight, you're right. It is, for most prospects, our one opportunity to welcome a new pilot to the august ranks of aviators. Those who don't become pilots will forget soon enough. But those who elect to fly will be grateful for a lifetime.

With this in mind, our job at the intro lesson is to demonstrate *why* each prospective customer should become a pilot, with just enough attention to "how," to answer their questions. In other words, concentrate on the benefits, not the process.

Years ago I remember my Dad telling me, as my brother and I helped him clean grease off the bottom of his airplane, "This sure is a lot of work, for a rich person's sport!" We laughed, and continued scraping. None of us doubted that it was worth it; my Dad flew us all over North America, and on one occasion shepherded his Cessna 310 to Europe and back, suffering an engine failure on the return trip. If someone had implied to my Dad, back when he first visited the airport in 1949, that he'd probably spend more time cleaning bugs off airplanes than flying them, he'd probably have bought a new car instead. And that would have been a shame.

OBJECTIVES OF THE INTRODUCTORY FLIGHT

Perhaps the best way to address what must happen at an intro lesson is to consider what each prospect must take with them out the door afterwards. If you're ever to see them again, they need to carry away some specific impressions, preferably close to their hearts.

Adventure—"It Was Fun!"

It's generally agreed these days that the competition for student flight training dollars comes from other leisure-time activities, rather than other flight schools. In other words, your prospect has the urge to get involved in something new and exciting. If not flying, it could be boating, golf, snowmobiles or sports cars.

How will the decision be made? Of course there are many factors, but prominent among them are "Which one will be most fun?" "Which will give me the most lasting enjoyment?" and "Which will offer the best value for my investment?"

Knowing the possible competition should give you and the rest of your flight school staff some guidance on how to prepare for it. Sure, visit the flight school across the way and see what's going on over there. But more importantly, check out those other places your prospective flight training customer is likely to evaluate when seeking a new hobby, such as the boat dealer, the auto showroom, and the country club. *They* are the competition.

The intro lesson needs to be fun, with the promise of further adventure once prospects earn their certificates.

Remember, anyone who comes to the airport *wants to be convinced* that flying is a great activity to get involved in. That's why you need to "wow 'em"—impress them with all the neat things they can do once they become pilots. These folks may know nothing about flying, so you need to tell them *everything*.

What can you do with a private pilot certificate? Where can you go? Who you can take?

Although I received the following in the form of a letter, rather than at the airport, it clearly spells out the sort of customer purchase decision we're dealing with at the introductory lesson:

> "Dear Sir,
>
> I am hoping you could help me with my decision on whether to learn to fly or not. I am an Annapolis, MD resident, and am just about to put my sailboat on the market. Part of my reason for wanting to sell the boat is what is scaring me away from flying… boat was great at first but now it just sits at the dock. I find that like many hobbies picked up, the allure fades after a few years.
>
> I have asked pilot acquaintances for some of the more practical uses for being able to fly. The responses I have received are not very positive:

1) There aren't many practical reasons to learn to fly. The only use you could get would be if you actually owned the plane, and knew it and your flying ability well enough to fly to different areas of the country.

2) It will cost approximately $3,500–$4,000 to get my license, and most people seldom fly after a few years. (this sounds just like my boat…)

Do you have any advice that will help me figure out whether this is for me??…I have heard so many mixed reviews about flying…too expensive, wonderful, time-consuming, exciting. You can see my dilemma."

As you can see, this fellow is not asking *how* to get his pilot certificate, but rather, *why*. Although he asks for "practical reasons" to become a pilot, what he clearly wants in this case is assurance that it's worth doing in a broader sense, because he'll experience fun and adventure, and because being a pilot will give him lasting pleasure in ways that other activities cannot. To convince our prospects we need to offer examples. Here's the reply which helped sell him on flying:

"I am delighted and honored that you wrote me with this question. Over the years I've flown extensively both on pleasure and in the course of business.

With family and friends I've piloted light airplanes to the out-islands of the Bahamas for snorkeling, and to Gimli, Manitoba to witness a total solar eclipse. I've flown to Nantucket Island off Cape Cod, Catalina Island off the coast of Southern California, and to Mackinac Island at the confluence of the Great Lakes.

I've flown with my family over the Grand Canyon and through Monument Valley, gone sightseeing over Manhattan, and viewed the U.S. Capitol and Washington Monument from above while landing at Washington National Airport.

Several years ago I flew my family to Alamosa, Colorado to ride the Cumbres and Toltec steam railroad over the Continental Divide. We've been to Tombstone, to Santa Fe, and to San Diego. This spring my wife and I visited friends at a remote ranch in the beautiful mountains near Nogales, Arizona.

For years while living in Central Indiana we flew every holiday to Northern Illinois and Wisconsin to visit relatives. Bundled up with our holiday gifts in a Piper Cherokee or Cessna 172 we cruised right over Chicago and all the holiday traffic below.

I haven't yet mentioned the flying I've done for business, like from Indiana to Washington, DC in three hours. Columbus was an hour and a half, Buffalo and Kansas City, two and a half.

I also haven't mentioned the beautiful sights I've seen from the air, like the glow of snow-covered fields at night, the glory of sunset over city lights, and circular rainbows atop layers of stark white clouds.

By now I suspect that you're either impressed as heck or laughing hysterically. But I have to tell you, after all those years of flying, I still get the same big thrill with every takeoff.

Flying is great adventure, yet very safe if you use good judgment. I've grown immeasurably through the experience, and have had the joy of introducing flight to innumerable friends and associates over the years. And among the greatest pleasures has been meeting the caliber of people who participate in this activity. Those who fly for pleasure and personal business are an independent and successful lot. I've made my training money back many times over through business contacts made through general aviation.

There are indeed people who fly for a few years and stop. Usually it's because they either don't experience the joy, or they don't perceive that they have enough travel destinations. But if you talk to such folks you'll find that even they rarely have any regrets about having done it.

Incidentally, despite all my enthusiasm I must predict one disappointment you will experience once you've learned to fly. No kidding, you'll be sorry that you didn't start flying years sooner!"

I'm Already Well On My Way to Becoming a Pilot!

Remember, the objective of each of your prospects is to *be a pilot*, not a student. So anything you do to make them feel like they're already on their way to that objective helps bring them back. It's almost as if they will have "wasted" a lesson, if they don't go on.

Since our purpose is to sign up new students for flight training, it's very important to emphasize the concept of the introductory *"lesson,"* rather than an "introductory flight," or "demo ride." This is because one learns something at a lesson, whereas on a "flight," one is only a passenger.

While being a passenger is perfectly fine for customers buying sightseeing rides, that role is no good for selling flight training. Again, prospective students must finish the flight knowing that they can indeed personally fly an airplane. Otherwise they're not likely to come back.

There's only one way to make first-time fliers feel like pilots, and it's straightforward enough: *They need to leave the lesson knowing they personally flew the plane.* And they need to feel they now understand some of the mysteries of flight that not everyone knows.

I Flew the Plane (Here's Proof!)

If you can provide your prospects with proof that they personally flew the plane, to share with their friends and family, that's even better. These folks want to brag about it when they get home! That's why you need to memorialize this special event in a way that it will be remembered, and will ideally help enthuse family members about each prospect's future as a pilot, as well. To accomplish this, the prospect must be provided with keepsakes to take with them out the door. First, and most obvious, is a logbook *with the first entry documenting the flight.*

Even non-pilots know how important a logbook is. They know that every pilot has one, and that it's a treasured possession. (What they do not yet know about is the CFI's "secret weapon," the insidious affliction associated with every logbook which causes its hapless owner to develop an irresistible urge to fill in all blank spaces with entries!) Insist that the proud new owner of the logbook fill out name and address on the spot, to legitimize the entry.

Secondly, the prospect must be provided with something that can be prominently displayed at home or office, such as a first flight certificate. This certificate must be really "cool-looking," and *it must be framed*. After all, our objective is to get it on the wall somewhere where it will be an unavoidable reminder, not put into a scrapbook or stashed in a drawer to be forgotten two days later.

Finally, keep an instant camera loaded with film at the airport. At the end of each "first flight," snap a picture of your aspiring pilot — not in the flight school office, but in front of the airplane he or she flew, or in the pilot's seat. This photo may be mounted in a sleeve in the back of the logbook, attached to the framed first-flight certificate, or installed in a nice mini-picture frame of its own. As with the other mementos, it must be made into a lasting reminder.

This Is a Great Place to Learn to Fly

Next is the issue of how prospects feel about your facility, staff, and above all, the reception when they came out to sample flying. The objective is incredibly simple in principle, yet we in aviation have a long history of not getting it right. Running through each prospective pilot's mind when leaving the airport should be these thoughts: "These folks were glad to see me. I'll enjoy working with them, and they'll treat me right." Let's go a step further with that...

"I look forward to seeing them all again next week when I come out for my second lesson!"

Granted, some of this is in the hands of others at your flight school. (*See* Chapter 12.) But if you as instructor have any doubts as to whether your prospects will get an enthusiastic reception when walking in the door, then you'd better make a point of being there when they arrive so you can make it happen yourself.

Planes are Cool, and I Want to Fly Them!

This issue has never been an easy one, but it has become especially tough over the last few years, as the general aviation fleet has aged. Your prospect probably drove to the airport in a very nice car, perhaps a BMW, a Cadillac, or a Lexus. Aircraft expectations for such people often run to a jet, perhaps, and certainly something with a luxurious leather interior, at minimum. Unless you train in some very nice aircraft, your prospects will be hard to impress. There are several factors you can control of in this equation, however.

First, schedule your introductory lessons in the nicest aircraft on the flight line. Take the trouble to make sure they're clean on the morning of the flight — make sure all old pop cans are removed from the seat pockets! The condition of the airplane is important not only because of the message conveyed to the customer about quality, but also because a sharp-looking plane appears safer and more exciting to fly.

Also, many of us are conditioned to steering new students to the least expensive aircraft we rent. Part of your preflight questioning should address what sort of aircraft a prospect would prefer to take lessons in. Many flight training customers can easily afford to train in something they perceive as classier than the basic training aircraft. So spend a few moments on the ramp showing them what's available, and let them make the choice as to what plane they might prefer to train in. If there's a clear preference, why not do the intro lesson in that model?

MAKE THE INTRODUCTORY FLIGHT A SUCCESS

Now that we've defined the objectives of the intro lesson, let's follow the process through with a "typical" prospect. We'll assume that a pleasant, fiftyish woman, Wanda Soar, shows up at the airport for an introductory lesson (it could as easily be a seventyish man, or a twentyish student).

What is that person looking for? And how can we fulfill her expectations? I'd like to tell you that I know the specific answers, but I don't. Nor do you. No one knows why that lady is here, except for her. That's why, after graciously greeting your new guest, the first step is to offer her a comfortable chair, have a seat, and ask a few good questions. The first one is deceptively simple:

"Why are you here?"

We know Mrs. Soar has some interest in becoming a pilot, or she wouldn't have come to the airport. But what are her individual, unique reasons for wanting to learn? Does she love to travel? Is there a cabin in the mountains she wants to visit on weekends? Does she aspire to the U.S. Aerobatic Team? Is she a camera buff who wants to shoot photos from above? Perhaps Mrs. Soar has a business two hundred miles away, and is sick of driving there.

Mrs. Soar's answer to this simple question is critically important, because it tells you exactly what this prospect's experience today should be. Does she expect to learn the practicality of flying? Or the adventure? Does she want to experience thrills? Or to be convinced that flying is routine? The answer is different for everyone, so without knowing what each introductory-lesson customer expects, you're just shooting in the dark on the intro ride. (Incidentally, it's perfectly okay to take notes, just ask first.)

Once you've got that first answer, it's time to dig a little deeper:

"Mrs. Soar, please share with me three things you plan to do with your pilot certificate, upon completing it." This question, of course, will probably overlap the first one to some degree, but that's okay. The objective is simply to learn more about how she sees herself using her soon-to-be pilot skills. Be sure to encourage prospects to list all three, even if it takes a while—in the course of this discussion you will learn a good deal about their objectives, schedule, and perhaps even financial parameters. If they stop after giving you only two uses of their pilot certificate, encourage them to continue, by asking for a third.

The next question helps to define both Mrs. Soar's level of interest, and also her specific scheduling objectives:

"Mrs. Soar, by what date would you like to be a licensed pilot?"

Her answer will give you insights into how urgent her interest is, and how often you should recommend she fly. It will probably also make clear when she plans to start. The possibility of meeting a prospect's specific scheduling objective is a tremendous plus in selling lessons. Hopefully this woman will tell you, "I'd love to complete my pilot certificate by June, because that's when we've scheduled our family vacation...Do you mean that may actually be possible?"

"You bet, Mrs. Soar. June is almost five months away. If you are available to fly regularly in the meantime, it's entirely possible that you'll be able to fly your family on vacation."

The next question is, "If you knew you'd be a licensed pilot tomorrow, and had access to an airplane, what would you do?"

If you're getting the idea that these questions are somewhat similar, you're right. The objective here is to ask "why do you want to be a pilot" in as many different ways as possible.

Pay close attention to every answer, ask follow-up questions as appropriate, and then be prepared to demonstrate, on the ground and in the air, how flying fits their objectives. *If you listen carefully, your prospects will tell you at the intro lesson, very specifically, how to sell them flight lessons.*

LET'S FLY!

So what happens on the flight, itself? First, it's important in the spirit of a lesson, to spend a little instructional time on the preflight. "Don't expect to understand everything today," you should tell prospective pilots, but then proceed to explain a few basics — flight controls and the primary instruments. As you show them around the aircraft, casually mention some safety features, such as the fact that most aircraft systems are redundant.

Again, we want the prospect to come away knowing something they didn't when they arrived. We also want to remove a little of the mystery, so they'll be more confident about their ability to quickly master flying in future lessons. Just be sure to keep your explanations simple — discussion of Bernoulli's Principle at the intro lesson will scare half your prospects away.

How much hands-on flying you allow each prospective student to do obviously depends on factors like weather, traffic, and that person's confidence, but ideally you should be sure that prospects fly enough turns, simple climbs and descents that you can "vector" them back to the vicinity of the airport prior to landing. The objective is to make the conversation back home go something like this:

"Hi Honey, how was flying?"

"It was fantastic! Can you believe it? I actually flew the plane *myself* for almost the whole lesson. It's surprisingly easy!"

Making the conversation go that way takes a bit of work on your part. First, if there's any doubt about the weather, you've got to muster the nerve to postpone the flight. If it's bumpy or windy, or if visibility is less than seven or eight miles, you're not going to accomplish anything by flying except to scare someone away from taking lessons.

Next, there's the adventure value of the flight. Not only must each prospect feel that he or she flew the plane, but if you can incorporate any sort of special experience, that's even better. Check out a nearby lake, fly over your prospect's home, or view a nearby city.

"Hold on," you're saying, "How can I do a lesson like that in only twenty minutes, and without charging ground time, to boot?" To which your manager adds, "How can we make any money if we exceed twenty minutes on an intro flight?"

These are legitimate questions, to which there are no easy answers. One must either give an adequate introductory lesson, recognizing that the economic objective is to cover the cost by selling subsequent lessons; or, alternatively, charge enough for the intro lesson so that it can be done properly without the flight school losing money.

One way to deal with this problem is to offer several options to the customer. The scenario might be something like this: Let's say Mrs. Soar brought with her an introductory lesson coupon. After interviewing her, you determine that her ultimate interest is in using her pilot certificate for travel.

She seems a bit nervous, but has always wanted to fly. Clearly she's enthusiastic, but needs a smooth and uneventful flight emphasizing the utility of flying for the travel she wants to do.

"Mrs. Soar," you tell her, "we have several options for today's introductory lesson, and of course your coupon can be applied toward any one of them. We can go up for a short flight in the local area, for the face value of your coupon. Another option is to take a full one hour first lesson, against which we'll apply your coupon. That will give us time to explore the area a bit, and allow you to do more flying. The third option is to take a short flight out toward Fish Lake, where your cabin is. Even if we don't actually go all the way out there, we'll be able to see the lake, which should give you a good idea of just how close your cabin really is by air."

"You mean we could actually fly to within sight of the lake, yet this afternoon? How much would it cost?"

"Yes Ma'am. Fish Lake is hardly more than a hop, skip and a jump, in flying terms. Since we don't have to deal with traffic in town, or drive that windy road out to the lake, we can be within sight of the lake very quickly, plus we'll have plenty of time to get you acclimated to the aircraft along the way. If you'd be comfortable investing about sixty dollars in addition to the coupon, we can really demonstrate the benefits of your pilot certificate for getting your family out to the lake."

As we discussed earlier, you may forget this intro lesson by next week, but for the prospective pilot it's a big deal. Make it really special, and you've just created a budding new pilot.

One School Redefines the Intro Flight

With all this talk about the adventure of flying, here's what one flight school is doing to redefine the "demo ride" in a whole new light.

Dorothy Schick, of TakeWING, Incorporated in Eugene, Oregon, has masterfully re-packaged her company's introductory lessons into "Adventure Flights," targeting specific audiences.

classicFLIGHT
TakeWING incorporated

A fun flying adventure!

Experience the excitement

of piloting an airplane

Before you do the usual...

DO THE UNUSUAL!

Been there? Done That? Try this! Taxi an airplane to the runway, call out the final check list and then takeoff to an exciting scenic flight over the beautiful Eugene/Springfield valleys, buttes and rivers. **Oh, and did we mention, you get to fly the plane too!**

Challenging, incredibly exhilarating, and yes, even mind expanding. So, before you pole, pedal, paddle, walk, jog, or java with friends, TakeWING with us!

Your ClassicFLIGHT package includes:

and a discussion of what makes

WomanFLIGHT
TakeWING, incorporated

Flying adventures for women

ready for change, challenges,

and new horizons.

It's time to: get fit, de-stress, invest...
and CHANGE YOUR LIFE!

WomanFLIGHT is exciting, fun, and yes, even life changing. You'll experience what it is like to sit in the front seat of a small aircraft while viewing the beauty that surrounds us...**oh, and did we mention you get to fly the plane too?**

Three Adventures to Choose From:

The Smith Adventure—**Elinor Smith** flew under four Manhattan bridges at the age of 17, the Mayor grounded her for 10 days. *30 minute flight* **$95**

The Scott Adventure—**Blanche Stuart Scott** was a brilliant pilot who was denied a job in 1916 because of her sex. *45 minute scenic flight including a touch-and-go (landing with immediate takeoff).* **$115**

The Barnes Adventure—**Florence (Poncho) Barnes** was a hard talking free spirit who did stunt flying for Howard Hughes' film *Hell's Angels*. *One-hour scenic flight plus demonstration of nonacrobatic aircraft maneuvers and touch-and-goes.* **$125**

All Flights Include:

➶ A hands-on preflight aircraft inspection along with an explanation of the airplanes instruments and controls.

➶ A guided lesson on how to taxi the airplane.

➶ A breathtaking aerial tour of the areas cities, valleys, rivers and buttes.

➶ Flying the airplane! Under the guidance of your pilot, you will feel what it's like to hold the controls and FLY!

➶ A sparkling cider reception, WomanFLIGHT certificate plus two Polaroid photos: One in the pilot's seat, and one in front of the airplane—thumbs up, of course!

TakeWING, Inc. brings the dream and enchantment of flight to you through customized flight training experiences. All flights depart from the Creswell Airport (10 minutes from Eugene) and may be delayed or rescheduled due to weather conditions. A liability waiver is required prior to participation. For more information about our AbleFLIGHT, KidFLIGHT, ClassicFLIGHT or our small group programs please give us a call.

Reach us at 555-9464

Dorothy Schick, president of TakeWING, Inc., is a licensed commercial pilot and certificated flight instructor. She is an active member of the 99's, Airplane Owners and Pilots Association, and Experimental Aircraft Association.

Does this flight sound like fun, or what?! By highlighting the little things which make flying special, Dorothy has succeeded in presenting the introductory lesson as the great adventure it should be. It's easy to see how the concept of adventure flight guides the expectations of both customer and instructor as to how the ride will be conducted.

Perhaps most innovative about this approach is the way it presents the intro lesson as an excellent value for the customer, while allowing the operator to charge a fee which actually has room for profit. (For another TakeWING Adventure Flight example, *see* Chapter 13.)

SCHEDULE THE NEXT LESSON BEFORE YOUR PROSPECT DEPARTS

Most of us are appropriately sensitive about pushing people to do something they're not interested in. But again, your "first flight" customers are interested in flying, or they wouldn't have come to the airport in the first place. What they expect you to do is help them get started on something they really want to do—become a pilot.

So your specific objective at the end of this introductory lesson is to schedule the next one.

There will of course be prospects who, for whatever reason, are not ready to schedule their next lesson. Of those folks you must ask, "When would you like to proceed with your pilot training?" Once they've answered, request permission to call them, if you don't hear from them by a specified date; then make a point of marking that call-back date on your calendar in front of them.

Be sure to ask for a business card, or otherwise record the prospect's address and phone number. You'll need that information to keep your prospects hot for future flying lessons, using the methods discussed last chapter.

By now you should be getting the message that the customer should never be allowed to shoot right out the door after the flight. If at all possible, the objectives should be to debrief them after the flight, make sure any remaining questions are answered, present them with their mementos, and agree on a plan for future action.

Hopefully that means scheduling a lesson, but at the very least it means establishing a follow-up date. In this case you'll send them a thank-you note, and then call to answer any lingering questions about the experience. Remember that your customers will be fully satisfied only if they leave the airport knowing *exactly* how they will continue their flying adventure.

Six

A Professional and an Expert

If you've been flying for long you already know that, given similar training and experience, there is relatively little difference in piloting ability between competent aviators. As much as most pilots like to think they have exceptional flying skills, the fact is that very few perform measurably better than their peers in the cockpit, and also only a handful have skills much below those of the general pilot population.

This means that pilots must generally compete for flying opportunities, not on the basis of piloting ability, but rather on attributes like personality, motivation, and especially, professionalism. So not only is professionalism important for making a positive impression on others, but it is the key differentiating factor between one pilot and the next. The image that a pilot presents to others may well be the single most important issue impacting the success of his or her career.

This professionalism issue affects flight instructors as much as other pilots, if not more so. As a CFI, your ability to attract students, to retain their business, to get them back for additional training, and ultimately to move on to other aviation endeavors, all rests heavily on personal professionalism.

Professionalism and Recruiting

Pilot candidates tend to have differing objectives, budgets, and desires. Some go for instructors who push them hard, while others prefer gentle and compassionate teachers. But in at least one respect, every student seeks the same type of flight instructor—an expert—someone who really knows aviation, can communicate it well, and makes learning easy.

Regardless of which type of prospective pilot you may be courting on a given day, to attract students you must come across as an expert. If you learn tomorrow that you need a major operation, you'll look for the best doctor, right? For an impending court case you'll seek out the sharpest attorney, won't you?

Flying may not seem like such a big deal to those of us who are already pilots, but to the average new flight student, flying an airplane seems as daunting as surgery or a court case. After all, he or she is going to invest significant time and money in an activity many people regard as dangerous.

For these reasons, each of your prospects wants to hire the best, sharpest, and most knowledgeable instructor available. In fact, for the largest number of potential pleasure pilots, lessons will occur only if and when they stumble onto that "ideal" instructor, the one with the right chemistry, the expertise, and exactly the right amount of confidence.

An Expert in the Eyes of a Student

Even if you are new at instructing, your training and experience certainly qualify you as an expert, compared to the students you're training. But how does one come across as an expert? The main thing to realize is that most of your prospects aren't qualified to judge your credentials. Rather, they'll measure your expertise by personal qualities. Does this instructor look and act like a professional? Does he or she communicate well? Will he or she be confident and comforting in the alien environment of an airplane?

Your personal demeanor has more impact on the perceptions of your prospective students than your actual flight experience. What can you do to develop your image as an "expert"?

Look Like a Professional

One unavoidable indicator of professionalism is appearance. No matter how impressive your piloting skills, you've got to dress nicely, keep your hair neatly trimmed, and your shoes in good repair. Piloting a plane is perceived by the public as an activity of precision, professionalism and exactitude. The more you look like the sort of person who has those qualities, the greater your success will be in attracting students.

The average flight candidate doesn't want to get into a little airplane with someone sporting a ring through the nose and a torn T-shirt. That's not saying such folks can't be talented fliers…just that they don't fit the image anticipated by the average would-be pilot.

Your prospective students are a diverse bunch. Some are romantics who seek to soar with the birds. Then there are the would-be F-15 pilots who routinely fly their flight simulator jets to landings on virtual aircraft carriers, with turbulence set to "ten." Other aspiring pilots are more interested in the practical travel aspects of flying. All of them want to train with someone who seems more or less like an off-duty military pilot.

If you want students you'll have to play the game of dressing for success. Skeptical? Wear a white blouse or shirt with tie down to the flight school and see what happens. Prospects walking in the door will gravitate immediately in your direction; the boss will aim more of them your way, too. And don't be surprised if you feel more like a professional, yourself.

Act Like a Professional

Now that you're looking sharp, let's consider speaking skills. Teaching is a high-level communication activity, and so is selling your services. Since it's hard for potential clients to evaluate your technical expertise, they'll base their decisions largely upon your ability to convey ideas clearly and professionally.

If, like so many of us, you feel uncomfortable about your abilities to meet and talk with people you don't know, now is the time to do something about it. Speech classes, drama and debate groups, and sales seminars are all great places to develop verbal communication skills.

A less formal route for those who wish to improve their speaking skills is to join the terrific organization known as Toastmasters, International. Toastmasters has local chapters in just about every town big enough to support an airport, and costs very little to join. Each chapter meets once or twice a week, often in the morning over coffee and doughnuts. Participants take turns speaking extemporaneously, usually only for a minute or two at a time, with feedback from the group. It's fun, and quickly improves your verbal communication skills in a no-pressure environment. Another good reason to attend: it's exactly the sort of group where you're likely to meet prospects for your flight instructing services.

Keep in mind that improving your communications skills will not only make you a better instructor, but will also help with your future flying career, especially when it comes to professional pilot interviews.

One key aspect of professionalism is really knowing your stuff. After all, that is what you are selling to your students. This means not only staying sharp on your knowledge and flying skills, but also concentrating on your own training with the same energy you put into teaching your students.

With that in mind, make it your objective to take your own training only from the very finest instructors available — not the easiest, not the least expensive, but the best.

Along with earning additional CFI ratings from quality instructors, take advantage of every other opportunity to learn from their expertise. Having trouble teaching holding patterns to your students? Ask for permission to observe a lesson on the subject given by the best IFR instructor you know.

The Words of a Professional

Those of us in aviation have developed some very bad habits, when it comes to choosing the words used around potential flight students. I once worked for a guy who'd go ballistic whenever any of his employees used certain expressions in front of a customer. Comments like "Let me play around with this problem and see if I can solve it," literally threw him into tantrums.

"We're in a professional business," he'd yell, "and our job is to *work* to solve our customer's problems, not 'play around!'" I can assure you that my coworkers and I quickly learned not to use such phrases around customers or our boss. While his concerns seemed a little silly to us at first, we quickly grew to respect the fact that our boss was right on target; using proper language in front of our customers impressed them with our professionalism, thereby increasing their respect for us and their comfort with our work.

As we talk flight training with non-pilots, we have to be equally careful in our choice of words. There are the obvious no-no's, like joking about the "controlled crash" made by your last student, in front of a prospective customer who just showed up for an introductory lesson.

But there are also some less obvious terms and phrases which can have tremendous impact upon students and potential customers. Here are a few things which should never be said:

"I'm building hours for the commuters." This one sentence has probably cost instructors more students than any other words in the history of flying. Most CFIs say this sort of thing all the time, without even realizing that what they're really telling their flight students is, "My purpose here today is to use *your* money to pay for *my* flight hours so *I* can move on to a better job."

I kid you not. Just watch as some well-meaning CFI utters this ultimate *faux pas*. The color drains from the faces of every flight student within earshot, sometimes accompanied by grinding teeth and clenched fists.

Our students are investing their hard-earned money for one purpose only, to learn aviation skills from already-professional pilots. They don't want to hear that their instructors are at the bottom rung of the industry ladder, and they certainly don't want to pay for our flight hours.

Please keep this in mind, next time you discuss your future career plans. It's perfectly okay to build professional experience as a flight instructor. But "building time," or "building hours" should never cross your lips, especially in front of a student.

"Flying is expensive." Compared to what? Don't ever assume that flying is too expensive for your customers. It may well be too expensive for *you*, but most of your flight training customers can easily afford it. What every-

one is really concerned about is *value*. Most flight students, if not taking flying lessons, will happily spend the same money or more on something else, like speed boats, snowmobiles, or golf. Bought any lift tickets at the ski lodge lately?

Flying is a terrific value. Where else could someone invest a similar sum of money, and get lifelong, year-round joy out of it?

"You'll need to spend about a hundred bucks for your flight review." Notice that I used the word "invest" when talking about the terrific value of flying, a sentence or two ago. Money which has been spent is gone forever, but an investment by definition is intended to produce a return. Becoming a pilot is an excellent investment; money and time are devoted to generate something of lasting utility and personal satisfaction.

If you do your job right, your flight students will earn excellent returns on their flying investment in the various forms of pleasure, personal achievement, and perhaps financial rewards if they go on to flying careers.

So tell your student she'll need to *invest* a minimum of two hours in her flight review. Don't ever use words like "spend" or "cost," when talking about flight training. Your services as a professional should be an excellent investment. If they are not, than you truly are just building time. And who among us wants to fall into that category?

"Here's my student, Joe." Let's talk "students" for a moment. As we've previously discussed, people don't sign up for flying lessons because they want to be students. They enroll in the program to be pilots. So from a terminology standpoint, it's best to avoid introducing your students as, simply, students.

Most people who invest in becoming pilots have already achieved some measure of success in life. And just about everyone learning to fly hopes to earn additional respect as a pilot. So referring to someone as "my student" in front of others, often makes people squirm in their shoes (especially folks like doctors and professors). And making people uncomfortable is bad for business.

A better approach is to say something which implies accomplishment, rather than student status. "Meet Joe. We're working together on his Instrument rating," or, "This is Beverly, our next Private Pilot." Or, "Irv just joined the ranks of cross-country fliers today."

Actually, if it didn't fly so much in the face of convention, I'd prefer to use the word "client," rather than student. As you know, professionals like attorneys and accountants refer to their customers as clients. Not only does the term imply delivery of personal and tailored services to an individual, but it is extremely respectful. Since our relationship as instructors to our flight students is very similar to that enjoyed between other professionals and their clients, I think the word client would be a terrific term for us to use in describing our students.

In any case, from here on I encourage you to think in terms of clients and investments when dealing with your students and prospective customers. Using this terminology positions you as the true professional you really are.

EARNING THE RESPECT OF YOUR STUDENTS

As a friend of mine who manages a very successful flight school puts it, "Instructors who put their students first have the most students; therefore they build flight experience fastest."

Earning the respect of your students begins with some very elementary habits, including meeting your scheduled appointments, operating within the rules, and honoring your obligations.

Most flight students must structure their lessons around work or other activities, so scheduling takes effort and planning on their part. By showing up for your appointments on time and prepared, you demonstrate the same consideration for them that you'd like in return. In fact, one of the best ways to motivate students to arrive prepared is to do it yourself.

Next comes the importance of operating within the rules, meaning everything from federal regulations to those of your flight school. Everyone needs rules to live by, and when one begins breaking them, life quickly becomes confusing. Primary students need black-and-white procedures to structure their decision-making, and the easiest way to teach them is to follow the rules. If a required instrument isn't working, don't fly. If the visibility is below school minimums, do a ground school session. Not only will this approach earn you the everlasting respect of your students, but it could very well save their lives in the future. A pilot's attitude about whether or not following the rules is important is most certainly set in primary training.

Finally, it is absolutely imperative for instructors to meet their obligations to their students. As you instruct you'll be faced with constant pressures in many directions. The temptation will often exist to rush students through training in order to get on with something else. Resist the urge! Canceling or reneging on short notice for reasons other than health or an emergency is such a severe affront to your students that most will never forget it. No matter how great that just-came-up multi-engine charter opportunity may sound, don't take it if it means bumping an obligation.

Any time your student shows up at the airport and you're not there, the ramifications will eventually catch up with you. No kidding, it's entirely possible that you'll meet this student again one day when he or she is on the hiring board of an airline where you're applying, or has bought a jet and is looking for someone to fly it. Having been fired is also a very serious blot on a pilot's record, and at most flight schools not meeting student obligations is a darned good way to learn about it.

Look at it this way. If you get invited on a charter once, it's likely to happen again. And since the charter department is likely to be impressed by pilots who meet their scheduled obligations, saying no may actually result in more flying opportunities for you later.

Of course, the time may come in your career when other opportunities and obligations become more important to you than your students. That's okay, providing you don't allow your changing priorities to get in the way of their training. As soon as you see your potential to get busy with other things, start planning for the transfer of your students to another instructor you respect. By handing your students off gracefully, you'll be able to pursue your own goals without hampering the achievement of theirs. And that's the only way it should be done.

Take the Judgments and Concerns of Your Students Seriously

There will always be occasions when your students question you about the safety or correctness of a situation you personally find acceptable. When they do, you simply must take their concerns seriously. As an instructor it's easy to unilaterally make decisions about what's important and what's not.

"Don't worry about it. That nick you found in the prop is no big deal."

But when a CFI brushes off such a question, dangerously negative messages are transmitted to the student, like "it's not important," or "you won't understand." Of course, that's not necessarily why the CFI is making the decision, but this message is sent all the same. If your student becomes concerned about a nick in the prop, take time to explain why you're not worried about it. If the student is still not convinced, bring out a mechanic to take a look at it. By taking your students' concerns seriously, you are empowering them to command their own aircraft in the future.

Another good reason for addressing your students' concerns is they may be right. One of the great learning experiences of my own flying career came early in my instrument training. I was taking IFR lessons out of a small field near Indianapolis, and had arranged with my instructor, "Dave," to fly an IFR training flight one night over to Champaign, Illinois. The plan was to fly over in a Cessna 172, pick up a friend who was coming to visit, and return. The flight would be about a hundred miles each way, and with approaches at each end, would make an excellent lesson.

Before leaving work, I phoned Flight Service for a briefing. The surface weather sounded perfect for the mission, 700 – 1,000 overcast along the route, with excellent visibilities underneath. Winds aloft were strong from the west. There were reports of turbulence, however, and surface temperature was reported in the low forties.

When the briefer got to pilot reports, I quickly became very concerned. Icing had been reported by many aircraft, including several "moderate icing" reports by airliners. Even to a novice like me, this clearly did not sound like a good evening to go flying in a 172.

But when I called my instructor and reported the weather to him, Dave pooh-poohed my concerns. "It's well above freezing at the surface," he observed, "so we can always descend into warmer air, if climbing on top won't do the trick." I was only ten or fifteen hours into my IFR, and he was a seasoned Aerostar pilot. Who was I, to question his judgment?

We met at the airport after dark, picked up our clearance, bundled into the Skyhawk, and took off. The instant we entered the clouds, ice began to accumulate. By the time we reached our filed altitude of 4,000 feet, the leading edges were coated with a growing ridge of ice. As I tried to concentrate nonchalantly on my VOR tracking, Dave peered out the window into the blackness with his flashlight to monitor the accumulation.

"We'd like 8,000," he told ATC, who promptly cleared us to climb. The ice continued to build, so Dave again queried the controller. "Where are the tops?" A few moments later word came back, "there's an aircraft at niner who says he can see the moon occasionally, figures tops are at ten or eleven thousand."

By this time our little 172 had struggled up to 6,700 feet or so, and was finished climbing. The level of the tops had become academic. We continued to chug along through the soup, blackness perforated only by the intermittent glow of the rotating beacon reflecting off the inside of our personal cloud. Although we were carrying full power, the airplane soon began to very gradually lose altitude.

"Dave, don't you think we ought to go back?"

"Yeah, well, I guess so."

He dutifully notified ATC of our decision to return, and requested 3,000. As we made our one-eighty and began serious descent, the plane started shaking dramatically.

"Just some ice on the prop," said Dave.

We broke out mercifully soon over the airport. Due to the strong westerly winds aloft, we had covered very little ground during the outbound leg of our journey, then had rocketed back within minutes, thanks to the tailwind.

The windshield being almost totally iced up, I made my approach at ninety knots while peering out through a two-inch diameter peep-hole melted by the defroster.

On short final enough ice cracked off the prop so the vibration almost stopped, and after a bounce or two we were on the ground. My knees would barely support me when I climbed out. The 172 carried leading edge ice approaching three-quarters of an inch in thickness, along with large chunks remaining on the prop and the still mostly-glazed-over windshield. There was nothing pretty about it, and I had plenty of time to ponder the experience during the drive over to Champaign to pick up my friend.

Now any pilot reading this story should recognize the sheer stupidity of taking off into such conditions, and even as I try to put myself back into the shoes of a novice instrument pilot it's hard to imagine that I went along with the idea.

What a way to learn! Imagine how much more effective it would have been for Dave to have gone over the weather reports with me, issued an "attaboy" for a no-go decision well-made, and taken me out for a cup-of-coffee ground school session instead.

Every instructor must be aware of the phenomenal impact of his or her decisions on students, and the examples those decisions set. Had Dave's overconfidence not resulted in such an obviously serious situation, I might have been misled into trying something equally dangerous on my own, in the future. And maybe things wouldn't have worked out the same way.

Don't Be Intimidated by Students Who "Know More Than You"

Taking this concept one step further, it's imperative to retain command of your aircraft even when your student is the one who's "more experienced."

I know I'm not alone in having undergone some stress, early in my flying career, when I allowed "more experienced" pilots to effectively command the plane I was supposed to be instructing them in. That ended for me when two airline pilots almost busted Class B airspace with me on board. The two of them had just bought a twin several hundred miles away, and not being current in singles, asked me to give them dual in one of our flight school Pipers to pick it up. Since they were airline pilots, I figured they knew everything, but they didn't. Neither had flown VFR in years, and they were clueless about recent airspace changes. They couldn't read a sectional chart very well either, I learned. At that point I vowed never again to let anyone else interfere with my judgment when I was in command, no matter how experienced they were supposed to be.

I've since come to learn that it's quite common for high-time pilots to arrive at the airport for rental checkouts, expecting to skim by on the weight of their logbooks. In fact, only two jet pilots I've ever instructed took a light-aircraft check-out seriously enough to prepare in advance. Neither had flown a light airplane for years, so each had gone to the trouble of studying the Cessna manual ahead of time, memorizing relevant airspeeds and weights, and arming themselves with good questions about systems and procedures.

Maybe it sounds like overkill, but was I impressed. Both of those guys are true professionals.

SEVEN

Tricks of the Trade

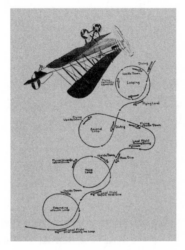

As with most things in life, experience brings new perspectives to flight instructing. Along with improved teaching skills and new insights into motivating your students come some harsh realities and a few disappointments.

The single most important thing for a beginning flight instructor to understand is that no student is perfect. Just like us, every student faces his or her own challenges, and makes his or her own mistakes. As long as you understand that, and make identifying those challenges part of the game, things generally go along pretty smoothly.

Here are just a few insights on the process of transferring knowledge and judgment to your students.

ENCOURAGE INDEPENDENT ACTION WHILE MAINTAINING CONTROL

Along with teaching aeronautical knowledge and flight maneuvers, our mission as instructors includes development of some much more subjective skills in our students. The ability to make good decisions, maintain confidence and presence of mind in difficult situations, and to apply good personal judgment when there's no clear course of action: these are all marks of a good pilot.

Not long ago an instructor friend called to boast about one of his students who, during his very first solo flight, had shown the presence of mind to divert safely to another airport after a plane became disabled on the runway he had departed from.

Then there was the time when a student of my own encountered roughness and then lost engine power on his long solo cross-country. He trimmed for best glide, picked a desert clearing, and began circling down. As he proceeded with his carefully-memorized emergency checklist, the engine roared back to life. You've guessed it — the problem was carburetor ice — despite clear Western skies on a seventy-degree day.

Sure, each of these students did exactly what he was supposed to do, but too many pilots err when the pressure is on. I'll bet neither one of these students knew he had it in him, before it happened. How do people develop the skills to handle unexpected circumstances like these?

There are no easy answers to this question, but a huge part of preparing people to handle such situations is to give them the freedom to make their own mistakes during training. Sure, tell them ahead of time the proper way to execute a maneuver, and share with them the broad perspective on how and why it's done that way. Then let them make their mistakes — and recover on their own.

Too many flight instructors, in their zeal to show each student how to "do it right," never allow the student to learn from doing things the wrong way. In fact, the most receptive students are the ones who have tried something themselves, and can't make it work. Let them make mistakes, and then take advantage of their concern about the outcome to get their attention and *really* teach them something. They may not have listened to you the first time, but now that they've screwed it up, they are all ears.

"Sometimes mistakes are dangerous," you say. That's most certainly true. Let students wallow in their mistakes only when it can be done safely. When an error cannot be allowed to follow its course for safety reasons, take your student to an environment or an altitude where it *can* be done safely, and then let them goof up there. But let them see it through; allow each student to find out "what will happen if...."

All students need to know that they can and will make mistakes. Knowing that makes them cautious, and confidence that they can make a mistake and recover without your help allows them to deal with unexpected problems when they do occur.

DEVELOP JUDGMENT ALONG WITH FLYING SKILLS

Among the most difficult skills to teach flight students are judgment and decision-making. Obviously, major portions of these attributes come from the background, character, and confidence of each student as a person. And as we'll see later, sometimes already-developed student traits or attitudes make it difficult to teach judgment or decision-making at all.

But the good news is that for most flight students judgment and decision-making skills can indeed be enhanced, at least when it comes to aviation. And when you succeed in improving someone's ability to make a decision under difficult circumstances, you've done something to be proud of—those skills may very well benefit them for the rest of their lives.

How does a good pilot decide whether to take off, when the weather is marginal? When the weather is good, or really bad, the decision is pretty straightforward. But it's those marginal days that make pilots bite their nails.

As tough as it is for someone having plenty of experience, how does a new pilot learn to make such difficult decisions?

The answer, from a flight-instructing standpoint, is teaching of two interrelated principles: first, evaluate every situation from the broadest possible perspective, and then build a plan based on options.

The Role of the Big Picture

Richard Collins, of *Flying* magazine, once wrote a marvelous article about the importance of "the big picture" in instrument flying. In his commentary he compared two kinds of pilots; one carries a three-dimensional picture of the surrounding environment in his or her head, and mentally keeps track of where the aircraft is relative to that environment at all times. "Situational awareness," many pilots call it.

The other type of pilot flies each instrument procedure "like a worm in a tube," treating each step in the procedure as a "now I make a right turn, then I make a left turn" direction-following exercise.

Both pilots can complete the procedure, and to the outside observer there may be no apparent difference in their performance. But if something goes wrong, or if an unexpected decision needs to be made, it's a pretty good bet that most of us want to be riding with the pilot having the big picture, not the one in the tube!

Understanding the big picture can indeed be taught at every phase of training. In making piloting decisions, the student needs to learn to gather every bit of available information, and to compare and relate every bit of it before drawing any conclusions. Comparing information from multiple sources generates that big picture, by filling in blanks with understanding that may prove valuable later.

So in teaching weather decisions, for example, you've got to work with each student through every bit of information that's available, compare it, and then put it all together. What's the relationship of the actual surface weather to the forecast? Do winds at given locations confirm the position of a front shown on the map?

And how do reported in-flight conditions compare with those predicted in the Area Aviation Forecast, SIGMETs, or AIRMETs?

Understanding the big picture may, if a given pilot decides to go, allow safe and confident decisions en route, should any surprise adverse weather be encountered.

The same principles apply whether you're teaching emergency engine-out procedures, mountain flying, or power-on stalls. Spend the time to make sure students understand the big picture, and they will more likely find themselves equipped to handle whatever may come their way.

Options: the Key to Defining Risks

Once students understand the big picture, for a given situation, consideration and development of options is the next decision-making step. In general, the more options a pilot has available in a given situation, the lower the risk of catastrophe. By constantly considering options for every flight situation, you can easily develop an invaluable decision-making ability in your students. This needs to be done both for planning purposes, and for every phase of flight.

"Before we takeoff, let's consider what we'll do if the engine fails just after we lift off. What would be our options?"

"If the weather deteriorates on your cross country, what will you do?"

"If headwinds are stronger than forecast, what will be your course of action?"

"If your destination airport is closed, then what?"

Do this long enough, and your students will start thinking that way themselves. Then you've really accomplished something in their performance as pilots.

Now back to that VFR pilot weather decision. Let's assume with our student that weather at the departure airport is fifteen hundred overcast with visibility seven miles, marginal for VFR flying.

Once the pilot has gathered and processed all available weather information, and has equipped himself or herself with the "big picture," it's time to take the next step, which is to evaluate options. If the pilot takes off on the planned trip, and has problems, how many options exist, and what are they?

Obviously if the weather is fifteen hundred overcast, or lower, for hundreds of miles in every direction, that VFR pilot is likely to have nowhere to go after take-off given the possibility of encountering deteriorating weather. No options equals no-go.

But let's say there are numerous closely-spaced airports along the route, the terrain is flat with no obstructions, and weather along the first portion of the route is consistently reported at fifteen hundred overcast, with improvement forecast to begin at any time. Now there's at least one option if the weather deteriorates, which would be landing along the way. Maybe this trip is feasible after all.

Suppose the pilot is northbound, and the forecast calls for rapidly improving weather from the west. Based on comparing forecast and actual reported weather the pilot determines that the weather is rapidly improving to the north, and that clear skies already exist only a few miles to the west. How does that sound? If the pilot doesn't like the weather after takeoff northbound, he or she can turn west and fly directly into clear skies. All of a sudden fifteen hundred overcast doesn't sound so bad.

To confirm that all these signs do indeed add up to a safe palette of options, the pilot runs out on the ramp and interviews another who just flew in from the north. "Heck," says the inbound pilot, "ceilings are already up to five thousand, just six or seven miles north of here."

The point is that any time your student has no options, or cannot evaluate them due to lack of information, there is only one course of action—don't go. But by identifying several safe and comfortable alternate plans, pilots can rationally and safely generate a justifiable "go" decision.

The Difference Between Regulations and Responsibility

Before we close the door on decision-making, there's one last thing on this topic which must be conveyed to your students. Students spend a great deal of time studying regulations, in preparation for both the knowledge and practical tests. Based on the way that regulations are written and studied, it's all too easy for pilots-in-training to conclude that if they're conforming with the regulations, they are safe. As anyone who has been flying awhile knows, that assumption could hardly be further from the truth. Be sure, when covering such material with your students, to differentiate and clarify between regulatory minimums, and safe practice.

"Okay, James, you need to know that the regulations require that you have completed three night takeoffs and landings to a full stop within the past ninety days, in order to carry passengers at night. Remember, however, that those are just the legal minimums, not nearly what any prudent pilot would require of himself before flying after dark with passengers. I recommend...."

INSTRUCT BEYOND THE MINIMUMS: HAVE FUN IMPARTING YOUR KNOWLEDGE

All too often instructors get into the rut of performing only lessons in the flight training syllabus. We may have to conform to the syllabus, when it comes to the order of events and not skipping anything, but there's no law against teaching something additional to your students. So have some fun! Offer "special" lessons when you see a learning benefit.

Among such special opportunities might be gusty-crosswind days, regionally-specific situations, such as mountain flying or travel to high-traffic airports, or perhaps an extra flight for an instrument student when conditions are particularly unusual, educational, or challenging.

Advise your students of the benefits, when such opportunities come up, and give them the option of investing in an "extra" lesson on a special topic; they'll go for it much of the time. When it's all over, those "special" lessons are the ones students often remember and appreciate the most.

TRUST 'EM BUT WATCH 'EM

The importance of allowing flight students to make and learn by their mistakes has been discussed above. Over time you'll get more and more comfortable with each student's performance, knowing that the likelihood of serious errors declines with every lesson.

However, no matter how great any student may be, don't ever allow yourself to become complacent when someone else is flying. As is the problem with airborne emergencies in general, students rarely depart from what you expect them to do. As a result, it's hard to maintain preparedness for when something does go wrong. And you can never predict what anyone else is going to do in a given situation.

Over some fifteen years of instructing, I only remember a few scares when students did something dangerously unpredictable, but those were indeed memorable. One of the best flight students I've ever had quit the controls during a night touch-and-go on a narrow runway edged by snow banks. I'll never know why the otherwise confident student picked that moment to stop flying, but in any case I grabbed the controls barely in time to avoid clipping a wing on a snow bank.

Then there was the time when an older pilot receiving a flight review let go of the rudder just at the buffet, while practicing a power-on stall in a 210. We instantly entered one of the most vicious spins I've ever encountered, putting us in test pilot territory. Fortunately I was able to promptly recover uneventfully.

One of the more unusual in-the-air surprises presented to me by a student makes for a rather entertaining story. Ron Jones, I'll call him, was a middle-aged fellow who co-owned a pristine Piper Warrior.

A would-be fighter pilot, this guy actually wore a military flight suit with Nomex flying gloves to instrument flying lessons in his Cherokee. (No kidding!) Despite, or perhaps because of the unusual outfit, Ron proved to be an outstanding IFR student. He arrived thoroughly prepared for each lesson and had exceptional powers of concentration, which made for performance far better than the average instrument student.

Ron was a neatness and organization fanatic well beyond the actual flying of his plane. On any given Saturday he'd be out there vacuuming the interior, touching up the upholstery, and polishing away microscopic bugs. This was a man who invested hours of every weekend cleaning the seams and rivets on the underside of his airplane using a toothbrush, and who disassembled the instrument panel for the sole purpose of cleaning seams where invisible bits of grime might accumulate.

Ron and I breezed through his instrument training with very few problems, and I found myself consistently impressed by his rock-steady flying under the hood. Clearly, if the guy was going to dress like a military pilot, he also intended to fly like one, and I certainly couldn't fault him for that.

When the time came for Ron's IFR cross-country, we decided to make the trip something special. We waited for a good IFR-flying day, loaded up the Warrior's back seat with Ron's teenage son and his son's friend, and took off for Kalamazoo, Michigan to visit the warbirds museum on the field.

The flight up was uneventful. We got a good deal of actual IFR, and as usual, Ron was organized, thorough, and unflappable. We then spent several hours at the museum, heading across the street to consume hot dogs at a nearby bowling alley before taking off for home.

The weather had deteriorated a good deal during our visit to the museum, so we endured a wet and bumpy ride on the next two legs—a perfect training environment for a soon-to-be instrument pilot. We shot our second required approach at South Bend, and then headed for home.

As we approached our home airport, we were cleared for a straight-in VOR approach. As usual, Ron organized his approach charts well in advance, studied them yet again (he always pored over the likely approaches before coming to the airport), and tuned the radios.

We passed the initial approach fix; Ron made the radio call requested by approach, and we began our descent towards the stepdown altitude. I clearly remember cruising in the right seat, feeling fat, dumb, and happy, and taking pride at that moment in our joint performance: both my student's excellent flying, and my own expert instructing.

Obviously, I wouldn't be boring you with this long story if something interesting wasn't about to happen. We were established in a relatively high descent rate several hundred feet above the stepdown altitude, in the clouds and about ready to begin level-off, when the only disaster that could possibly phase the unflappable Ron Jones occurred.

I guess the combination of greasy bowling-alley hot dogs and two hours of bumping around in the soup hadn't done much for the two teens in the back seat. First one boy and then the other began vomiting violently all over the new upholstery. As soon as Ron realized that someone was puking all over his pride and joy, he turned around and began screaming at the boys. Situational awareness out the window, Ron gripped the yoke as he turned around, rolling the plane immediately into a steep bank, and rapidly accelerating our rate of descent. Had I not grabbed the controls immediately, we would have plummeted right through our stepdown altitude.

I tried twice to get Ron back on the controls, but the man was so flustered that, as I remember, I had to complete the flight. Throughout the approach, landing, and taxi to the ramp, Ron continued berating the boys and attempting to clean up the mess. I guess he wasn't unflappable after all.

After we shut down and the boys got out, I turned to Ron.

"Ron," I said, "Now aren't you glad that happened?"

"What do mean?" he asked, still red-faced with anger, "We just finished re-upholstering those seats."

"Ron, what did you learn from this experience? Do you realize what might have happened if I hadn't taken the controls?"

"Yeah, I should never have let what was happening take me away from flying the plane."

"So Ron, aren't you glad it happened?"

"Yeah, well, I guess I am," he said.

"Let's go in and talk about it over a cup of coffee." I said.

Like so many hard lessons in airplanes, if you live to tell about it, you'll never make that mistake again. With students, it's extra-important to make these errors a great learning experience, by doing a thorough debriefing, including an extended "what if…" session.

In this particular case I learned a lesson or two myself. One, as we've discussed, was being reminded again of the importance of staying alert, no matter how well things may be going. Although I had been closely following our progress on the approach, I was so comfortable with Ron's performance, and so surprised when things fell apart, that I didn't react as quickly as perhaps I could have.

The other lesson was one instructors rarely experience. The student had been so outstanding in his general performance, that I had no concept (nor perhaps did he) of how he would react to a surprise disruption. From that day on, whenever I have an *apparently* unflappable student, I make an effort to create a few minor emergencies on my terms…just so I can see what happens.

THE ART OF DIAGNOSIS

In many respects a really good flight instructor shares the attributes of a talented mechanic. If you've had much experience working with mechanics, be it on airplanes, cars, or other devices, you know that the mechanic's hourly rate is not the main measure of what a repair will cost. Rather, the charge is most closely tied to how quickly the mechanic can identify what is wrong. A really good mechanic uses some combination of experience, knowledge and intuition to get quickly to the heart of each problem. Once the true problem has been identified, it's easy enough to effect the repairs. Less-talented mechanics may have to replace many parts before solving the problem. The art is in the diagnosis.

Flight instructors face many of the same challenges. When a student reaches a learning plateau, a good instructor grapples with the cause of the student's difficulty; then assigns one or more exercises to solve that specific problem. Sounds easy enough, but often it is not, since flying is such a complex operation.

When a particular student can't master landings, there are a hundred variables, any combination of which could be the cause. If your student doesn't begin to get the hang of it after a reasonable amount of practice, you've got to begin dissecting those landings to figure out both what's being done right, and where the problems may lie.

GET HELP WHEN YOU NEED IT

Being an independent bunch, we pilots like to think that we can solve every instructing challenge ourselves. As a result, you'll rarely hear instructors talk about the specific challenges they face with students. They may complain about a student's inability to master landings, but there's little discussion about the specific symptoms. If the landing problem doesn't cure itself after many repetitions, both instructor and student get frustrated, and it's no surprise to anybody when the student becomes traumatized and quits.

One of the keys to professionalism is knowing when to get a second opinion. Have you ever been around doctors? If you could visit the doctors' lounge at your local hospital, you'd hear plenty of shop talk. Sure, there's lots of conversation about hobbies, personal plans, and problems, just like in the CFI lounge. But you'll also hear a great deal of discussion about challenging medical cases.

"My patient has these symptoms. Any ideas about what the problem might be? How would you treat it?" It's nice to know that several heads are getting together when the medical problem is yours.

Soliciting a second opinion is equally important among instructors. One of your students can't master crosswind landings? You are definitely not the first instructor who's ever experienced that problem, so it's a very safe bet that some of the other instructors around have great tips on how to improve crosswind landings, all you have to do is ask.

"I've got a student who just can't deal with slips. Any suggestions on how to handle it?"

One way to open up these instructing challenges for discussion is to take advantage of weekly CFI meetings at the flight school, to get suggestions. Ideally, discussion of student problems should be a regular agenda item at each instructors' meeting. Going around the room, each instructor describes her or his instructing challenge of the week. The issue could relate to a specific maneuver, like spins or NDB holds; or it might be something more cerebral, like fear of flying or lack of confidence.

Then the group can discuss different ways in which each instructor's problem of the week might be addressed. As with all groups, there are always a few instructors who have difficulty gracefully accepting the suggestions of others. The trick here is one of attitude; each instructor should consider the assembly as his or her professional advisory group, one expert to another. It's not that you have to take anyone else's advice, but rather the objective is to collect ideas from the group, evaluate them, and then try the combination you think will work best to solve the problem.

When a student learning plateau can't be overcome within two to three lessons, it's time to get a fresh look at the problem. Just as any good doctor seeks a second opinion on tough cases, ask your student to take a lesson with someone you respect who may have a different method of tackling the problem. Tell each of them the truth; define the problem as you see it, explain to each that you feel that a fresh perspective may help in solving the problem, and send them flying with the specific mission of tackling it.

"Marsha, as you know I've been really pleased with your progress to date, but I notice that over the past few lessons you've become really frustrated with landings. That's no surprise, because learning to flare is challenging, and almost no one gets it right without quite a bit of effort.

"Anyway, I've learned that when one of my students shows signs of getting discouraged, one of the best ways to get back on track is to try a fresh approach. Remember Bill, who gave you your last stage check? I know you enjoyed flying with him, and he's an instructor I really respect. I'd like to suggest that we schedule your Tuesday lesson with him next week, just to get a new perspective on landings.

"Since Bill flies stage checks with so many pilots every week, he knows all the tricks in the book. He may also be able to reassure you that every pilot goes through this challenge in learning landings. A fresh approach to the subject should make you quite a bit more comfortable with your progress. Of course, you and I will be back to our regular schedule on Thursday."

Referring a student to someone else for a lesson may sound simple enough, but it takes guts, and as a result few CFIs do it. Some instructors find it most comfortable to refer such problems "upstairs," to a stage check instructor, the chief flight instructor, or perhaps a respected older instructor on staff.

In any case, don't make the mistake of assuming you can solve every student difficulty on your own. When a student's progress has ground to a halt, you owe it to everyone involved to try and solve it promptly. Not only is it to the student's benefit to have another instructor have a look, but also to yours. That's because failure to re-establish progress will sooner or later lead to the student quitting. Perhaps equally important is to consider that if the student has a really serious performance problem, perhaps one impacting safety, a second opinion may relieve you of sole pressure to make a difficult decision about that pilot's future flying.

A second opinion almost always makes the correct course of action clear. Get help when you need it.

Symptoms of a Problem Student

Almost every flight student sooner or later reaches some sort of learning plateau relative to some particular maneuver — that's just part of the learning process, and in fact it's really important to let your students know just how common it is, when they reach one. Fortunately, problems of flying skill can almost always be solved, given diligent instructing, a patient student, and occasionally, illumination of the problem by second opinion. In my own years of instructing, I have never experienced a student flying skills problem that wasn't eventually ironed out.

But certain types of problems are not so straightforward to address, especially when related to personal characteristics such as personality, motivation, or attitude. We're talking here about such problems as inability of a student to assume responsibility or take command, situations where a student has a flying problem but won't accept help in solving it, and even cases where an instructor begins losing control of training an aggressive student.

When these sorts of problems occur, successfully solving them can require all the skill an instructor can muster, plus extensive help from others. Unfortunately, these are also the kinds of student difficulties that occasionally cannot be solved at all.

When You've Just Got to Give Up On Them

Even with all this emphasis on helping your students over the hurdles, there are in fact situations where you simply must be prepared to drop a student. Anyone who has ever had to do this knows that it's a very difficult thing to do.

First, the student has very likely invested quite a bit of time and money before such a problem becomes apparent … and the fact that there is a serious problem of some kind means that probably the student is in deeper than most, financially, due to efforts to solve it.

Next there's the economics of dropping a student, as it impacts you and your employer. Not only are you going to lose a student, but your employer will suffer the combined effects of lost income, and perhaps, an angry ex-customer let loose on the community.

Finally, we all know the terrible effects of telling a person that they should not proceed with something they really want to do.

All these are excellent reasons why a good instructor will always seek a second, third, or even fourth opinion before allowing or suggesting that a student drop out due to a problem.

So what are the warning signs for a student who should not be flying?

Lack of motivation is a fairly common problem encountered among students. If the student simply won't prepare for lessons, and won't complete the assignments you have given, you may be fighting a losing battle.

I once had a student who simply would not take command of the airplane; all decisions of any kind were deferred to me, making solo flight out of the question.

Perhaps the most serious problems arise when a student consistently shows poor judgment, or proves to be downright foolhardy. Often these types show their colors early. You know the type — they want to do barrel rolls and loops on the intro lesson, but have no interest in learning all those boring basics.

Sometimes, though, you just have a nagging suspicion that maybe the student is going to do something stupid; on rare occasions, you won't know there's a problem until something happens.

The thought of one former student still makes me shudder to this day. The guy was a college student—I'll call him Phil—who had completed his first two solo cross-country trips uneventfully. Together we went over the planning for his long cross-country flight, which was to consist of three legs, each over one hundred miles in length.

On the morning of Phil's departure on his long cross-country, we checked the weather, which proved ideal for the trip, and confirmed details such as the agreed-upon plan to refuel at each stop, get his logbook signed, and so on.

Phil then took off on his flight, after which nothing more was heard from him until his return late that afternoon. In fact, nothing was heard from him then, either, because upon landing he quietly parked the airplane and went home.

The excitement didn't begin until the following morning, when a lineman noted a big dent in the leading edge of one wing on a rental airplane. The dent was a deep one, so the assumption developed that a truck or other vehicle must have run into it on the ramp overnight.

The next bit of news came from the refueler. "Hey, I thought you folks would want to know that the 152 out there was almost bone dry!"

"Which one?"

"The one with the big dent in the wing...."

That, of course, led to an investigation of who flew the plane last, which turned out to be—you guessed it—Phil, on his long cross-country. Phil initially denied his involvement, but since he was the only one who had flown the plane it didn't take long before the truth came out. When it did, I seriously contemplated quitting flight instructing forever.

Phil's mom was paying for his lessons, and it turned out that their arrangement was that the flight school billed his mom each month for his flying. Now when Phil landed at his first planned stop and went to order fuel, he was confronted by the incredible revelation that if the plane was refueled, he'd have to pay for it.

Phil did have a credit card with him, but decided that if he used it to pay for the fuel, his mother might not reimburse him. Of course he was faced with an identical situation at his next stop, too. So he did what only a cartoon character on a hangar bulletin board would do — took off without refueling — twice!

During the interrogation afterwards, I asked Phil if he had calculated the fuel required to get home, before taking off on the last leg of his combined four hour journey without refueling, to which he said something to the effect of "I figured I probably had enough."

Then, as my future flying career flashed before my eyes, he told me about the dent.

"I was taxiing around at one of the airports [couldn't remember which one] looking for the fuel pump [even though he didn't refuel]. There were some of those big light poles around, and I ran into one with the wing."

"Did you have a mechanic look at it?"

"No, I didn't tell anybody."

This guy had actually completed one or two flights of over a hundred miles each in a Cessna 150 with a dented leading edge, without refueling, to boot.

Needless to say, these events caused me (and my supervisor!) to look back at my training experience with Phil, and to try to figure out how I could have predicted his behavior before he'd risked his life, the flight school's airplane, and my career.

From the beginning, Phil had been a lackluster performer. First, he rarely prepared for his lessons ahead of time, so we spent an inordinate amount of time going over things he should have learned before coming to the airport.

Phil was also sloppy in every sense of the term, often neglecting to bring along items he needed for lessons, and routinely leaving candy wrappers, pop cans and other trash in the airplanes. It had also been difficult to get him to take seriously the preflight preparation and attention to detail that marks a good pilot. Phil did an adequate job flying the airplane, but was not inwardly driven to excel on the maneuvers.

In short, I'd been uncomfortable with the guy's attitude throughout his training, but since he'd completed all of his maneuvers and training requirements within parameters, I had tolerated his performance as passable.

The lasting lesson for me out of that experience was the absolute requirement for consistent good judgment on the part of my students. If it becomes apparent that they don't have the personality to do things right, I drop them. You will, from time to time, encounter flight students like these who can fly the plane, but have emotional or personality characteristics which aren't conducive to being good pilots.

When that happens you have very few options. The wisest thing to do, when you run into a student who perhaps shouldn't be flying, is to turn the case over to your chief flight instructor or flight school manager. Explain why you are concerned about the student's performance or capabilities, and let management determine the proper course of action...just be sure to do it *before* somebody gets into trouble.

EIGHT

Keeping Your Students Flying

We've spent a good deal of time up until now discussing how to convert prospective flight students into customers and addressing aspects of training them. But there's another factor in the equation. How do we keep those new flight training customers flying, not just through the private certificate, but over the long haul? Unlike retail stores, where just about any clerk can satisfy the customer with a modicum of service, flight training is delivered in a one-on-one, professional manner. As said before, that makes the role of the instructor in satisfying each customer similar to others who provide one-on-one services, such as attorneys, doctors and accountants.

So while a well-organized flight school with clean airplanes and a nice facility is certainly important in retaining business, a great deal of the responsibility for success or failure in the flight training of each student falls squarely on the shoulders of the flight instructor. The instructor must build a relationship with each flight customer, understand and meet that person's special needs, convey the necessary knowledge, teach the skills, and provide the motivation and encouragement required to finish. It's for these reasons that so much responsibility for retaining flight students must rest with the instructor.

Accordingly, we must never forget that our main reason for teaching is student satisfaction. Someone's paying for those lessons, and keeping them happy is what makes the business work. Students want to fly safely and proficiently, and enjoy themselves. As instructors, our part in achieving those goals is immeasurable.

COCKPIT MANNER:
TREAT YOUR STUDENTS LIKE FELLOW PROFESSIONALS

As discussed previously, our flight training customers want to be pilots, not students. Therefore one of the very best ways to enhance the satisfaction of your flight students is to treat them as equals. Your students want to do a professional job of aviating, whether or not piloting is the ultimate career goal. Keep this in mind and you'll know how your customers wish to be treated, both on the ground and in the airplane — "cockpit manner," you might say.

You can counsel a fellow professional, offer suggestions, act as a mentor, provide encouragement, and advance criticism in a sensitive manner. But expressions of frustration, disgust, or irritation must be avoided at all cost. You can't make fun of anybody's performance as a pilot. And it is absolutely destructive to express anger toward students under any circumstances.

This approach may sound elementary, but that doesn't make it less important. Along with the effect of discouraging students, anger and irritation from the instructor drastically erode student confidence. As confidence goes down, training progress ceases and the risk of error increases dramatically. So not only does directing anger at students drive them to quit, but it's downright dangerous.

Speaking of cockpit manner, my brother Alan once had a CFI who was a nervous wreck in the cockpit. This instructor was the type who continually wants to grab the controls away from his students, but to his credit he had apparently recognized this and developed a coping mechanism. Repeatedly during every lesson this guy's hands would shoot forward toward the controls — then continue in a smooth sweeping motion up to his head, where he would slick back his hair.

This repeated grab for the controls followed by grooming was so obvious that my brother was in stitches by the end of their first lesson together. By the end of the second lesson, however, Alan himself was nervous enough to start shopping for a new instructor. (One can only guess what he was doing to make that CFI so nervous.)

By treating each student as a fellow professional, you generate an aura of comfort and confidence which helps carry that pilot over the rough spots. Keep your students feeling like professionals through the ups and downs of training, and most all of them will complete the full course.

Proactive Instructing

We have all had teachers in school who simply showed up for class, taught their stuff, and went home. We might have adequately learned the subject from them, but never felt touched or personally motivated by their teaching.

Then there were the really special teachers who put their hearts into inspiring their students. It wasn't just a matter of putting in more hours than their peers, but rather, those teachers would reach out to every student in the classroom, with a genuine desire that every single one should love, understand, and want to learn more about the subject at hand.

These are the kind of teachers we as CFIs need to be — mentors, cheerleaders, counselors, advisors, and consultants. I like to call it proactive instructing: reaching out beyond the basic teaching to motivate and encourage our students, to anticipate and address their needs ahead of time, and to provide the support they need to keep coming back.

Learning to competently pilot an airplane is challenging, which is one reason so many students get discouraged and quit. Sure, the less-inspiring instructors may be perfectly capable of teaching students to be good pilots, but can they keep the less-confident ones flying? Can they inspire a level of enthusiasm about flying that gives each pilot the desire to continue learning and growing after the lessons are all over?

To keep all your students coming to the airport, take the initiative to keep them informed, confident, enthusiastic, and on schedule. The moment you let that support wane, a certain percentage of your customers will begin dropping out.

Tell Students Where They Are, How They're Doing, and What's Happening Next…*Every Lesson!*

Even if you do nothing else besides teach the syllabus, you absolutely must tell students *every lesson* where they are, how they're doing, and what's happening next in the schedule. Students are singularly unqualified to judge their own flight training progress, never having done anything like it before. So as a flight instructor you've got to take the time to lay out all the details of the training program, step by step, then show them where they are and where they're headed.

Each student must always understand what objectives remain to be accomplished to complete the certificate or rating at hand. This is because, by about two thirds of the way through training, students begin to seriously wonder if they will ever get done. Advise them regularly as to what remains to be addressed, so the end goal stays in sight.

"Good news, Jo…you are in the home stretch! As of today we have now covered everything required on the Private Pilot Practical Test; all that remains is to finish your cross-county requirements and brush up on your maneuvers in preparation for the test."

If you don't keep them updated, students start thinking they're not getting anywhere. Since you've covered steep turns for the last three lessons in a row, they assume that they're doing something wrong, and that training has ground to a halt.

A given student will actually come to the conclusion that, since she couldn't maintain altitude after the second try at steep turns, she will never be a pilot. No kidding, it never occurs to most students that what's challenging for them is usually difficult for everyone else, too. They tend to think that there's something wrong with their flying, and that the maneuvers are easy for all other pilots! That's why you've got to tell them repeatedly how they are doing.

Briefing your students about upcoming training challenges is equally important. Back in college and being hard up for money, I answered an ad for one of those "an hour of your time for $25" research experiments ... turned out to be in the psychology department. They sat me down in a chair and told me to stick my arm into a big bucket of ice water. The assignment was to keep my arm in there for as long as I could stand it.

It didn't take long before I became mighty uncomfortable, and removed my arm from the water. After a few moments' rest to get the feeling back in my arm, I was given my next assignment. This time, the experimenters would brief me first, then we'd see if I could keep my arm in longer. I was told in detail exactly how I should expect my arm to feel, starting with cold, then tingling, then numbness.

I then stuck my arm back in the ice water, and was able to keep it immersed in the ice water for about ten times as long as the first try. Now of course, you can't trust psychology researchers to tell you the truth about why you're doing an experiment, but I learned something all the same. When people know what's going to happen ahead of time, they can put up with a heck of a lot more difficulty than if they haven't been briefed.

This bit of understanding has helped me immensely throughout my instructing career. Take the time to lay out the program for your flight students ahead of time! Explain to students at the outset of training what to expect. Let them know that, during the first ten to fifteen hours of flight training, they should expect to feel challenged periodically while they're getting the hang of things, but from there it's on to solo and then pretty much clear sailing to the certificate.

Do the same thing before training each maneuver, and before the start of every lesson. When you start working seriously in the pattern, tell students *ahead of time* what to expect.

"Landings are fun, Justin, but they're challenging. Be prepared to complete four or five lessons in the pattern, before you start feeling comfortable with them."

Working with a new instrument student?

"We're going to spend the first ten hours on attitude instrument flying, with no approaches or radio work. The objective here is to develop basic control of the airplane on instruments. Then we'll add workload step-by-step, until you can handle additional tasks while flying, like timing and reading charts. You're going to find this challenging, because the whole point is to give you more to do every time you get comfortable. But, by the end of ten hours or so, you won't believe how natural it becomes to fly the plane on instruments while you're doing all that other stuff."

Then, when debriefing at the end of each lesson you can demonstrate each student's progress relative to the bigger plan. Continually let your student know where he or she excels. People tend to notice only what they did wrong on a given flight, so be sure to point out after every lesson all the things each student is now doing right.

"Sure, Bruce, you made a few wrong turns on Pattern A, but your altitude and headings were pretty much nailed throughout the lesson. You couldn't do that a week ago…Great job!"

Put the Decisions in the Hands of Your Students

One of the most difficult things to teach is judgment. Yet that is precisely the ability most needed for good decision-making in the cockpit. From day one, each of your students must feel at least part of the responsibility for safe conduct of the flight.

The trick to teaching decision-making is to put as many flight and operating decisions as possible on the shoulders of the student. When a decision needs to be made, think of yourself as a consultant. Your role in the decision-making process is to act as advisor and resource. But don't make the decisions yourself unless absolutely necessary.

Teach Your Students to *Fly* Like Professional Pilots

Want to impress your students from day one? We've already discussed the merits of treating your students like pros; the next trick is train each student from the beginning to fly like one. Even the most amateur hobbyist wants to fly like a professional. What constitutes professionalism in the cockpit? Good judgment and precision flying skills are certainly parts of the equation, which it is your job to teach them. But there's another factor found in most every commercial and corporate cockpit: consideration for the passengers.

The moment you start talking "passenger safety and comfort" with your students, you'll see an immediate change in attitude. They'll straighten up in their seats, arrange their collars, and assume a serious expression. Passenger considerations are the domain of professional pilots, and you've just asked your student to join you in those illustrious ranks.

Whenever you can, teach flying with smoothness, and pass along tips for alerting passengers about what to expect under various flight situations. It'll have a lasting effect both on the students you fly with, and on each of their passengers down the road.

It's amazing how much neat "passenger stuff" you can tie-in to the drudgery of learning new material. Working on cross-country? We've all heard the groans of our students (or soon will) when, on the first dual cross-country flight, we ask them to pull out the old flight computer and start calculating ground speed, fuel burn, and ETA (estimated time of arrival) for our destination. Students rarely believe any of this stuff is very accurate, so it seems like a time-wasting exercise to them.

I always use the opportunity to have a little fun…to work a little magic on my students' future passengers.

"You know, it's amazing how accurate this time, speed and distance stuff is," I tell them. "Now that we've leveled in cruise, we ought to be able to predict our touch-down time to within a minute or two. Your passengers will love it!"

Then, I pause for a moment to let the words sink in.

"'Touch-down will be at 16:37,' I tell my passengers. They never believe you can predict it so accurately. Give them a five or ten-minute window on either side, and bet lunch on the outcome."

Next thing you know, my student and I are figuring out which runway is probably in use at the destination, so we can factor pattern time into our calculated ETA.

Predicting turbulence before reaching it is another trick guaranteed to amuse the passengers. It also provides the instructor an opportunity to discuss indicators of mechanical and thermal turbulence...teaches the student to look ahead for the "bumps in the road," you might say. The student is less concerned about turbulence once the causes are understood, and so will be his or her future passengers. More importantly, the ability to predict locations of turbulence, updrafts and downdrafts can be a life-preserving skill, particularly in mountainous terrain.

Every Lesson Must be a Good Experience

If you think about it, few students are likely to quit flying after a great lesson. The occasions when it's possible to lose them are after "bad" lessons. What the heck is a bad lesson, anyway? Since we all know that making mistakes is one of the very best vehicles for learning, obviously a lesson where mistakes are made is not necessarily a bad lesson. The only really bad lesson is a discouraging lesson, one where the student leaves frustrated, disappointed, or demoralized.

So by making every lesson a happy one, you'll do a great deal to keep your students flying. That sounds a lot easier than it is, and requires quite a bit of work on your part, but you've got to do your very best to ensure that no lesson ever ends on a bad note. When a student leaves a lesson deeply discouraged, there's a measurable possibility that he or she will not be back.

When certain maneuvers on a lesson go badly, switch to something easy or fun to wrap things up. Be sure to suppress any frustration you may personally hold from the lesson, so the student feels that whatever happened there was no more, and no less than a great learning experience.

Build a Support Network

Along with encouraging students yourself, there are other things you can do to keep them rolling through the program. Many of the students who quit during training are types who don't communicate much with others; it should be no surprise that students without a support system are more likely to drop out. Therefore it's often valuable to introduce your students to each other, then encourage them to phone one another to share insights on everything from stalls to checkrides. Learning that another pilot finds many of the same maneuvers challenging always seems to help prevent discouragement.

It's also wise to make your students feel like part of the aviation community by encouraging them to join pilot associations like EAA (Experimental Aircraft Association) and AOPA (Aircraft Owners and Pilots Association), and to subscribe to general aviation publications like *Flight Training, Flying, Private Pilot,* and *Plane and Pilot.* Keep some subscription cards handy in your flight case. *Flight Training* is a particularly good magazine to start new students on right away; not only does it specifically address new student topics, but you as an instructor can issue free subscriptions.

You'll find that once magazines start arriving at their homes, students will begin peppering you with questions and comments about aircraft and issues they read about. It's also nice to have that additional aviation reminder arriving every month in the mail to reinforce their flying activities. If the student does drop out for some reason, that doggoned magazine just keeps coming month after month, hopefully tempting them to once again become involved.

Students Burn Out, Too!

Sometimes it's easy to forget why a student is taking flying lessons. For fun! For adventure! For relaxation! So when the flying ceases to be enjoyable for a student, especially over several lessons in a row, losing her or him to wind surfing or bungee-jumping becomes a distinct possibility.

For this reason, a good instructor must be very sensitive to a developing trend of discouragement in a student. Very often these problems occur when a student begins to believe that he or she can't master something. One way of addressing the problem we have already discussed — it's very important to keep each student informed as to their positive accomplishments, and where they stand in the process.

Another important element in avoiding discouragement is to continue to tackle learning plateau problems using a variety of different approaches, so the student remains encouraged that you're jointly on a road to solving them.

But when all else fails, and you see your student getting discouraged, it's time to take a break from those stalls, and make a pleasure flight. Remind them why they're taking lessons!

Think about it: Assuming your student doesn't have an aviation background in the first place, her or his experience with flying is pretty much limited to that first demo flight, followed by a series of very high-intensity lessons. Other than craning their necks for traffic, how many students get to relax and enjoy the view prior to solo cross-country?

But as we've discussed, very few pilots learn to fly because they love practicing stalls and steep turns. It may not be on the syllabus, but there are times when a casual "pleasure flight" lesson is the best thing you can do for your student. Fly to an airport twenty miles away for lunch. Make a trip to the nearest Automated Flight Service Station or radar approach control facility for a tour. Want to teach a collision avoidance lesson they'll never forget? Go to a pancake fly-in.

Wherever you choose to make this trip, allow some time at the destination to kick back and have a casual talk with the student. Very often, when students are given the chance to talk away from the pressures of the flight school, they'll open up and share with you concerns that have been frustrating them. Sometimes it's a personal problem, sometimes it's just student overload, but most often the problem sounds something like this:

"You know Greg," says your student, "I felt like I was doing great on the flying until we got to slips. But for some reason I just can't get those down, especially when it comes to no-flap landings. We've worked on them over and over and over, but I just don't seem to be getting anywhere. In fact, I feel like I've stopped making any progress on my flying at all."

We all know what that is, right? A learning plateau, something right out of the fundamentals of instruction. So what are you going to do about it? Keep working on slips, of course, perhaps with some new twists for variety. But here's a little something you can do right away to make that student feel better.

"I understand exactly how you feel, Jim," you say, "Every student, sooner or later in the course of training, reaches a point where the learning flattens off for a lesson or two. Sometimes it happens more than once. In fact it is so common that it has a name. What you are encountering is called a 'learning plateau.' Here, I'll show you."

At that point you pull out your dog-eared old copy of the *Aviation Instructor's Handbook*, open it to the appropriate page, and show that little graph depicting a learning plateau.

"Wow," says Jim, "You mean it's that common? I guess I've got nothing to worry about after all." Then the two of you can get on to something really important, like choosing between key lime pie or double-whammy chocolate layer cake for dessert.

The objectives with this sort of "pleasure flight" lesson are twofold: give the student some positive feedback on skills already learned, and remind them why it's worth the headaches to become a pilot. A round-trip cross-country flight of even an hour gives the student a chance to relax a bit, to look out the window, to track a heading and maintain level flight. Even by the third or fourth lesson, this is pretty easy stuff. If your student has been stressed out because he feels he can't master slips, odds are good that he's thinking, "I'm not making any progress." Of course you know progress is being made, but if the student can't do it perfectly there's a tendency for him to think, "I'll never get this."

So our little pleasure flight breaks the pattern of stressful lessons, and also gives you the opportunity to say, "Well, you may not have slips perfectly nailed yet, but look at how far your flying has come. You just hopped in an airplane and flew it comfortably for one hundred miles, all while holding your heading and altitude within private pilot practical test tolerances, handling the radios, and having fun to boot. Imagine doing *that* a month ago!"

In most cases the student returns from this "pleasure trip" encouraged, enthused, and rejuvenated.

Imagine the conversation following this lesson at home:

"Honey, guess what! I flew the plane all the way to Payson myself today! What a blast! I guess I got so worked up about the slips last week, that I forgot why I was taking lessons in the first place. Can you believe we could see all the way to Flagstaff? Even stalls don't seem so intimidating now. I can't wait until Thursday's lesson!"

Follow Up Personally When a Lesson is Canceled or Left Unscheduled

A big part of proactive instructing is recognizing the symptoms of someone who's thinking of quitting, and doing something about it before it happens. Instructors need to do this because very few people have the confidence and drive to overcome a serious challenge (or even a small one) without assistance from others. So for the vast majority of students, you must provide encouragement and support when needed to help your "client" complete the mission.

Let's say you're concerned that a particular student appears to be getting discouraged, and notice that the pilot's name does not appear on next week's schedule. There's a tendency to think, "when Jill is ready for her next lesson, she'll call me." That's certainly possible with some people, but often when students are just a little discouraged or lacking in confidence, and circumstances cause a lapse in the training schedule, they never come back.

Unless, that is, someone follows up and gets them back out to the airport. Sure, flight instructing is not supposed to be a personal counseling service, but as a teacher part of your job is to keep students motivated. And when it comes to flying airplanes, people sometimes need to know that their instructor out at the airport thinks they're doing great, and is eager to see them for another lesson—they need this to stay motivated.

It may sound funny, but many people quit flying because they think their instructors are unhappy with their performance. This perception is usually based on students being unhappy with their own performance, often accompanied by concern about not being cut out to be a pilot. And all this inner turmoil is often unknown to the instructor!

But just a call from the CFI, saying, "Hey Jill, we miss you! Come on out to the airport," usually makes students feel wanted, not pestered. It also demonstrates to the students that their performance has been perfectly satisfactory. Otherwise, why would you invite them back out?

Any time a student breaks the unwritten rules by leaving the airport without having scheduled the next lesson, it's time for you to put on your counselor's hat, make a courtesy call and help that student set one up. Sometimes it takes a friendly shove to keep students flying, but if we as instructors don't do it, nobody will.

Reward Students for Finding Your Errors

The flight instructor is always right...right? Well if that's not true, why do CFIs go through such trauma when caught in an error? After all, we're human, too. And the complexity of this aviation business is such that even the world's most experienced pilots are sometimes wrong.

So I challenge you, to challenge each of your students. Tell them that if they catch you in an error, and can prove that they're right and you're wrong, that you will do something special for them. Then nail down what that something special will be, like you'll buy them lunch at the airport restaurant, or give them an hour of CFI time at no charge, or let *them* cut the back of *your* shirt off, and put it on the bulletin board.

Making this sort of offer to our students may sound strange at first, but if you think about it, we *want* our students to catch our mistakes. We want them to think for themselves, we want them to scrutinize what they hear, to research the answers, and we even want them to be right sometimes. I'm not saying that instructors should intentionally make errors, but rather challenge our students to catch us making a mistake. (Of course if they're right all the time, maybe it's time to change professions.)

Nine times out of ten, when your student thinks that you've goofed up big-time, the two of you are going to get into one heck of an interesting discussion. (Anybody else in the area will join in, too.) In the course of the discussion the two of you will end up digging into the regs, the aircraft manual, the AIM, and whatever other sources are required to prove who's right.

The good news for your ego is that much of the time you'll be right. Sometimes there will be two correct answers, or two ways to interpret the same answer, so you'll both be right. That's not so hard to live with.

But every once in awhile your student is going to catch you when you're just plain wrong. That's the time to issue a pat on the back (as long as it won't constitute harassment), offer a handshake and congratulations, and pay up. I'm sure it's obvious that there truly are no losers in this sort of challenge — it keeps our students thinking and builds their confidence, while keeping us honest. Plus it's part of the fun of being pilots!

NINE

Priming Your Students to Pass the Test

As instructors, we must never forget that our number one mission is to help our students achieve their goals. A student's objective might be very clearly defined for accomplishment in a specific flight or two, like completing a flight review, a rental checkout, or perhaps an instrument competency check.

Then there are the wonderful but all-too-rare occasions when pilots approach you strictly with the desire to improve their skills...for help in polishing crosswind landings, brushing up on holding patterns, learning about mountain flying, or perhaps to try a hand at aerobatics.

These one-time assignments are almost always both fun and predictable for instructors; we get to run our own show, and to rely on our own judgment in determining when a student has met our personal training standards.

But the most common pilot training objectives are earning of new certificates and ratings, which means preparing each student for examination by a third party. Usually there's an FAA Knowledge Exam (written test) involved, and always there's the practical (flight test) conducted by an FAA inspector or a designated examiner.

The requirements for these tests are, of course, very clearly spelled out in the Code of Federal Regulations, test prep books, and published practical test standards (PTS). Your own education as a flight instructor focused on training your students to pass the technical requirements of those tests, and you will likely find yourself well-equipped to do it.

There are, however, a few tips worth sharing to help your students perform better on their tests in other respects.

THIS WILL BE ON THE PRACTICAL TEST

Every lesson you give to a student for a certificate or rating normally serves some objective toward preparation for a test, be it the knowledge exam or the practical test. Therefore one valuable instructing technique is to periodically refer to those upcoming tests, whenever you're covering something that's important to remember.

Did you ever have a high school teacher who used a "this will be on the test" signal? "Whenever I tap my pencil three times on the desk, you'd better write down what I'm saying; it's going to be on the test."

Preparation for the tests should never take precedence over teaching practical knowledge and flying skills. But referring to the expected performance of a maneuver on the practical test, helps students develop understanding and comfort about what they'll be doing there. By doing this, you can begin mentally preparing your students to perform better on their tests, from lesson one.

A private pilot student may not have a chance of maintaining plus or minus one hundred feet in altitude on her first try at steep turns. But by advising her of that objective right away, and at every practice thereafter, there certainly won't be any surprises at checkride time. The tolerances of the maneuver are as much a part of understanding it (for purposes of the checkride) as the basic flying skills.

At least mention those parameters when practicing each maneuver, and you'll take a good deal of the pressure off final preparation for the practical test.

FAA KNOWLEDGE EXAMS

For some reason, the knowledge test breeds more fear in many students than the practical. Maybe it's because it's the first test on any rating. Then there's the concept of taking a test administered by an agency of the *federal government*; for many private pilot students that's no less than terrifying.

Once students overcome the knowledge-test hurdle, they tend to be much more dedicated and confident about seriously preparing for the flight test. (Anyone who's had a student put off the FAA test until just before the checkride knows what I'm talking about.)

I suspect most instructors would agree that the best ground school learning results from a serious, in-depth classroom experience, taught by a seasoned and entertaining instructor. However there are always students who cannot or will not attend classroom ground school, for whatever reason.

Students who walk in cold to a force-fed weekend ground school may pass the knowledge test, but have little understanding or retention. And those who self-study using books, videotapes, or computer software often face challenges of self-discipline, understanding, and the ability to separate good-to-know background information from that specifically required to pass the test.

Personally I've found that the most effective way to deal with home-study students is to assign reading in association with each lesson, so that we can reinforce learning through discussion. For those students diligent enough to thoroughly self-prepare for the test, I assign practice tests out of the knowledge test questions; "answer every question which ends in '1.'," then "every question which ends in '2.'," and so on. We score each test to determine progress, then have the students answer all questions in areas where they prove weak.

After they have completed the home study, I give each student a practice test, recommend the sharp ones to take the FAA test, and then send less-dedicated and less-confident students to one of the national weekend ground schools to polish up and take the test. While not adequate as a student's sole ground school learning experience, those intensive weekend offerings do make excellent review sessions for pilots who've already done the reading.

My personal policy is to require that students complete the Private Pilot Knowledge Exam before starting the cross-country phase of training. By then the student has personally experienced most of the practical knowledge covered on the test, and at the same time learns basic cross-country flight planning skills by the time we're ready to use them. Besides, virtually everything on that test is important for safe travel outside of the local practice area.

Several weeks ahead of time, I identify a weekend ground school which would allow completion of the knowledge test just before our first planned cross-country. I then make a deal with the student that if the knowledge test is not passed before the scheduled ground school date, they will attend. This approach allows me to apply some serious leverage to get the knowledge test completed by the time I think it should be.

PREPARING FOR AN UNEVENTFUL PRACTICAL TEST

Preparing for the practical test is an entirely different matter than the knowledge test, for a variety of reasons. First, there's the need to understand aeronautical knowledge topics in depth beyond the simple answers. Next is the obvious aspect of performance—proficiently completing the tasks spelled out in the PTS. A third factor in successfully passing flight tests is attitude; the examiner will be looking for just the right combination of care and confidence. And finally, there are the potential effects of stress for the student to deal with. Beyond the specific items listed in the PTS, what can we do to prepare our students?

Get to Know the Examiner

As an instructor, it's easy to assume the attitude that other than scheduling students for their checkrides, there's no professional reason for getting to know the examiner. This could hardly be further from the truth. The examiner's rather challenging assignment is to determine whether applicants can competently and safely operate as pilots. How is this determined? Through the practical test, of course, but the better an examiner knows the circumstances and background of a given applicant, the more flexible and confident he or she can be while interpreting performance on the test.

As instructors, you and I are major components of each student's background. The better the examiner knows the instructor, the easier it is to interpret shades of gray on checkride performance. Sure, the examiner will do her best to be totally objective in judging applicant performance. But knowing that a given student has a sharp and thorough instructor, the examiner will be much more comfortable with tipping toward the student in borderline cases.

So make a point of meeting the various examiners in your area. When scheduling appointments for your students, spend a few moments quizzing the examiner about what he or she looks for on the checkride. You'll be surprised at how much most examiners will tell you about common errors and problems they see on tests. When you have legitimate training questions, call the examiner for interpretation, advice and suggestions.

A particularly good way to get to know your local designated examiners and FAA inspectors, is to invite them one at a time to speak before your flight school's weekly CFI meeting. In this forum examiners can share their personal testing philosophies, pet subjects and concerns, as well as recommendations for student preparation.

When you do schedule a student with an examiner you have not worked with before, interview other instructors and pilots about recent checkrides. It's also extremely helpful to have your students contact other pilots who have recently completed checkrides with the same examiner. Not only do those other new pilots share intelligence helpful in preparing for the practical test, but they can also help tremendously in reducing the stress on your current student by relating that the examiner was pleasant and easy to deal with, and expressing their comfort with the experience.

Brief the Student About What to Expect

After you've thoroughly covered all tasks students must know for the practical test, arrange for a brief extra session with each student, "to talk about the test." This is your opportunity to share a few observations which will hopefully set the mind of your student at least a little more at ease.

A Good First Impression

Sure, every examiner is supposed to be a totally objective individual, evaluating with clinical precision each applicant's performance relative to the PTS without regard to personality, circumstance, or conditions—superhuman, in other words. But examiners are people, too, and one needs to deal with them accordingly.

Just as when working with anyone you want to impress, it's worth the effort to prepare ahead of time with the objective of making a good impression. Any student who doesn't dress nicely for the checkride is just plain nuts. Examiners can wear anything they want to the test, because no one's evaluating them, but the student's objective is to convey competence, good judgment and professionalism. By walking in the door looking sharp, students create the expectation that they'll do a good job. That's a nice way to start any personal evaluation.

When preparing for a practical test, instructors worth their salt will obviously check out all of the required aircraft and pilot paperwork ahead of time. The practical test paperwork requirements are printed right there in that little checklist at the front of every PTS, and any instructor who doesn't go through it item by item with each applicant is looking for trouble.

Once you know it's all there, the next trick is to organize all of the paperwork your student will be carrying to the examiner, and make sure he or she has invested in some sort of appropriate flight case to carry everything in. (Doesn't have to be a $400 flight bag—just something neat, clean and organized, with no broken zippers, torn stickers, or dirt stains.) Take all the pilot paperwork, including a check for the examiners fee, and paper clip it together. Now do the same with the aircraft paperwork. Then advise your student to walk into the examiner's office and hand over that packet of documents and logbooks at the time of the initial handshake.

This simple act tells the examiner that the student is organized, and that the paperwork has been reviewed ahead of time. It also avoids the embarrassment and discomfort of sifting through wallet, flight bag and airplane looking for some errant document.

Next there's the airplane. Plan ahead for the day, and reserve the nicest trainer at the flight school; this is not the day to use the one that flies fine even though it has coffee stains and bubble gum on the seats. Not only must everything be in proper working order, but the airplane ought to be clean…makes the applicant look like the professional you have just trained.

Finally there is weather. The student will need to get a thorough briefing prior to the checkride and know what, if any, weather conditions might affect the checkride. He or she should be fully prepared to make any such concerns known to the examiner, and be prepared to make a go or no-go decision. The examiner expects to see decision-making, so every student should be prepared to unilaterally decide whether the weather is adequate or not, preferably on the conservative side.

Advise your student that after hearing and accepting a student no-go answer, the examiner may then decide that the weather is adequate for a checkride anyway — when that happens, the student shouldn't worry about it.

The Oral

The obvious key to passing the oral portion of a pilot practical test is preparation; if the student knows everything there is to know relating to the certificate or rating at hand, the oral exam is likely to work out just fine. It's difficult, however, for the student and the instructor to anticipate every possible question the examiner might ask. Those of us who have taken a few checkrides know that it's not easy to make it through an oral exam expressing the perfect answer to every question.

Your students will usually have two concerns about the oral. First is gaining confidence. After spending months studying all that material on everything from the regs to the Pilot's Operating Handbook (POH), and realizing just how much there is to learn, how can one confidently go in for the test? The second and related concern is, "What will I do if the examiner asks me something I don't know?"

Aside from the obvious techniques of quizzing the student in preparation for the oral, several other points can be covered in preparation.

It's important to make clear to your student well ahead of time that the oral exam is *not* a closed-book test. If you think about it, very few exams given in other environments allow the use of reference materials to answer questions during the test. Therefore the average applicant assumes the need to understand and memorize every detail of the entire aviation universe in preparation for the test. No wonder students are apprehensive!

Your students need to know that while the examiner obviously won't allow the whole oral to be read from a book, it's perfectly acceptable to look up occasional facts which don't come readily to mind. Emphasize that it's okay to say once or twice during the oral, "I don't know the answer to that one right off the top of my head, but I do know where to look." Not only does this relieve pressure on the student, but also it helps wonderfully to organize test preparation.

Since examiners generally recognize only FAA-approved publications as source materials for answering questions, have students prepare by familiarizing themselves with such materials as the regulations, the AIM, the aircraft's POH, and relevant advisory circulars.

A great way to accomplish this study is to have students buy adhesive tabs, then identify and mark key sections of each publication so they know where to find things. Of course in the process of figuring out where everything is, they can't help but learn a good deal of the material inside. The usual result of this approach is that nothing needs to be looked up at the oral, but if it does, the applicant knows where to find it quickly.

Applicants also tend to be more confident during the oral, knowing that prepared reference materials are available for backup, and they will be able to easily find answers to important questions during subsequent flying. Incidentally, there's one additional benefit to tabbing those books; even before the first question is asked, the examiner can see from the tabs that the applicant has put some heavy-duty work into studying the materials and preparing for the test.

Along similar lines, be sure students understand that it's perfectly okay to refer to keys and legends on aeronautical and performance charts during the test. Again, many people tend to think they're somehow cheating by looking at such references; that misconception could result in a pink slip.

In the course of preparation, it's helpful for the student to understand the general line of questioning at oral exams. Examiners are guided by the PTS as to topic, but not specific questions. So to cover the material, it's common for them to ask a general question or two on each topic, and then dig deeper into potential problem areas where the student's answers are weak. For this reason, it's important that the student have a broad understanding of the spectrum of topics, with additional concentration on problem areas.

Flying the Airplane

The beauty of today's Practical Test Standards, as compared to the ones used years ago, is that they so specifically spell out exactly what has to be done on the practical test, and to very specific tolerances. Instructor, student, and examiner all play by the same rules in this regard, and that's to everyone's advantage.

One problem faced by students, however, is that they view every one of those individual tight tolerances as a place to fail. The effect is similar to the guy trying to plug fifty leaks in a sinking boat with his hand—panic. Yes, each student must strive to perform every maneuver within tolerance. But it's equally important to understand that the overall objective of the examiner is to determine that the applicant can safely and proficiently operate an aircraft relative to the certificate or rating at hand. Each student needs to concentrate on achieving an *overall* good performance on the test.

Convey to your students that if they do a safe, thorough, and credible job, they have a very high likelihood of passing. Sure, examiners can fail students who wander one hundred feet off altitude, but they're not likely to unless the students are *consistently* off altitude and fail to correct.

The trick is for students to fly like professionals, doing their best on each maneuver without getting flustered by the details. Students also need to understand that examiners are concerned about the conduct of the entire flight, not just the PTS tasks. Perhaps the best way to explain this is to point out how many students fail to hold heading and altitude *between* maneuvers. And be sure that your students' habits include clearing turns, and otherwise safe and sensitive operations.

The next issue is conditions on the day of the flight. Among the biggest of student checkride concerns is ease of performing within the test standards, so the thought of taking their practical tests on a "bumpy" day is petrifying. We as instructors must explain to them that examiners have the latitude to flex a little on the tolerances, when justified by conditions. Students should do the best they can to remain within tolerances, of course, but if the flight is subject to thousand foot-per-minute updrafts, the examiner will take that into account. The fact is that in many cases it's easier to pass a checkride on a bumpy day — smooth conditions require a perfect performance!

Another important objective on checkrides is avoiding misunderstandings with the examiner. Students need to know that not everyone does every maneuver in the same way. Accordingly, they should not be alarmed if the examiner quizzes them about how they do a maneuver, and perhaps demonstrates a variation in approach. "Just listen carefully to what the examiner says, and ask follow-up questions if you don't understand," I tell them, "Don't get into an argument; just take the approach of, 'here's an opportunity to learn something.'"

Pilots must be highly experienced to earn examiner status, so the student has a special opportunity on checkrides to learn something. Most examiners also enjoy the opportunity to teach something extra. Tell students not to get concerned when the examiner starts teaching. Rather, take advantage of it and learn something.

Along this same line is the importance of having students clarify instructions from the examiner they don't understand. The time to avoid confusion is before executing a given maneuver, not afterwards. When in doubt, ask first.

Now for a tough one…what should your students do if they "goof up" in the airplane? There are two important points to make to your students in this regard. First, if they don't like the way a maneuver went, tell the examiner, "I can do a better job of that," and ask if they can do it again. Technically, examiners are not supposed to allow repeated maneuvers but hey, they're human too. In many cases the examiner will say, "Well, it wasn't perfect, but since you understand what you did wrong, let's move on." Or in other cases they'll say, "Sure, go ahead and do it again." Of course, if the student screws it up the second time, there's no way anyone can blame the examiner for giving a pink slip.

The other point that every student simply must understand is the number of applicants who fail checkrides because they were dissatisfied with how they performed a maneuver, thought they "might have failed" the test, and then proceed to completely botch everything else afterwards. Tell your students that, *unless specifically told otherwise by the examiner, they must assume at all times during the checkride that they are passing.* "If something goes poorly," tell them, "just move on to the next maneuver and put your full attention into that one." Point out to your students that if they do fail the test, it's customarily only required on the retake to perform the specific tasks missed on the initial checkride.

Therefore, completing the checkride with an overall good performance, even after perhaps marginal completion of a specific maneuver, accomplishes a good deal for the student. First, even though the student felt he or she goofed up, the examiner might have been satisfied, and doing the rest of the test well means the student passes.

Secondly, even if the examiner is unhappy with the performance of one maneuver, he or she may still pass the student if the rest of the ride went great, and the error wasn't too far out of tolerance.

Finally, by completing the checkride in good form, even a failing student benefits by likely limiting what will have to be accomplished on the retest, to only a maneuver or two.

Post-flight Your Student's Checkride

Just as with any normal lesson, your work as an instructor is not complete until you debrief your student after each checkride. This is important, because knowing how and what the student performed is useful in evaluating and improving your own teaching technique. If the student had problems on a specific maneuver, try to determine why, and whether it was a matter of the technique you taught, error of the moment, or a difference of opinion on how things should be done.

Another reason for debriefing is to get to know the examiner better, so as to more thoroughly prepare future checkride candidates. Most examiners don't view checkrides as creative opportunities. They do things pretty much the same way every time. Once you've thoroughly debriefed an applicant or two, you'll have a pretty good idea what to expect from each examiner, and how to prepare future students.

If your student failed the checkride, or experienced something other than "smooth sailing" in passing, it's really important to debrief the examiner, too. You'll find them to be generally frank about what the problems were (sometimes brutally so!) and how to solve them. They don't want to see similar problems repeated any more than you do, or your students. In addition to answering questions about the specific checkride, debriefing examiners offers another opportunity for you to get to know them better and further open the lines of communication.

Combating Checkride-Itis

Nobody likes to take tests, but by the time we get to flying lessons, most of us have learned to take them in stride. As you might suspect, college students and others young enough to remember the study and testing process from school tend to be tolerant of tests, if not enthusiastic. But the longer it's been since a flight student has experienced test-taking, the more nervous one tends to be about taking a test. In my experience the most challenging students to deliver to the examiner generally fall into two categories.

Successful people like doctors, lawyers, and business owners often have not been formally tested for many years, and aren't used to having their performance evaluated in any regard. Another group often concerned about testing is working people having relatively little schooling in their backgrounds. Don't be surprised if flight students falling into either of these categories postpone taking their checkrides for awhile.

When you anticipate checkride-itis ahead of time, there are a few things you can do to prepare nervous students. One is to have your student take one or more mock checkrides with the Chief Flight Instructor or another senior CFI at your flight school. The more "important" this instructor appears to the student, the better, since one objective is to improve the student's performance under pressure. Ask the senior CFI to give a formal and rigorous mock checkride, strictly following the PTS (Practical Test Standards), the objective being to expose the student to exactly what will happen at the real checkride, ahead of time.

Another helpful approach for dealing with nervous students is to arrange a brief social meeting with the examiner a week or two before the practical test. Ask the examiner to briefly explain how the test will be conducted, and what sort of performance he or she is looking for. Of course you will have already covered with your student the official test requirements in the PTS. But most students rest easier knowing that the examiner is a pleasant and normal human being, with a predictable plan in mind for the checkride.

Every once in awhile, you'll run into a student who is so traumatized at the concept of test-taking that unexpected behavior occurs at the checkride. When this happens it can be difficult and embarrassing for everyone involved. The trick for dealing with such problems is to work with the examiner afterwards to get the student over the hurdle.

In my own career to date, I have run into two particularly challenging instances of checkride-itis. Surprisingly enough, both occurred with Flight Instructor candidates.

In one case, I was working with a friendly and likeable young man pursuing a career with the airlines. As you know, the initial CFI practical test heavily emphasizes aeronautical knowledge, lesson-planning and teaching skills on the oral portion, followed by demonstration and teaching in the airplane.

This particular student was a good pilot in the airplane, and seemed to have good aeronautical knowledge in casual conversation. I quickly noticed, however, that he often seemed unprepared for lessons, particularly when he was assigned to teach a topic to me and other CFI students. Particularly odd was that the guy, while otherwise seeming to be diligent and honorable, would claim to have spent hours studying and preparing to teach such a topic, and then be totally unprepared upon our meeting.

Over time he appeared to buckle down, and when ready I recommended him for the practical test. I was disappointed when afterward he called to tell me that he had failed his test, but the bomb really dropped the next day when I talked with the examiner. It turned out that he had failed his oral, before ever getting to the airplane—he was unable to complete the weight and balance on a Cessna Cutlass. As you might imagine, the examiner was livid about having a CFI candidate fail on such a topic, and I was both horribly embarrassed and deeply mystified.

What was really bizarre was that the student himself didn't seem particularly disturbed about the whole experience.

The crack in the mystery came with a phone call the following night, from the student's father. "I just want to thank you," he said, "for working with my son and helping him so patiently with his flight training."

"Well, thank you," I said, "but I'm not sure I've done so well; you know he failed his Flight Instructor Practical Test yesterday."

"That I know," replied the father, "but let me explain a few things."

"Ever since my son was in grade school, he's had trouble taking tests. In fact the problem was so extreme that when he was younger, his mother or I sometimes attended school with him on test days, just to calm him down. Some of his other instructors have not been as patient as you; I just wanted you to know how much we appreciate your efforts. He is so close to reaching the first step of his dream career, and we know that you can help make it happen."

That call really set things straight for me. First I went to my flight school's Chief Flight Instructor and explained the situation. Together we came up with a plan, first encouraging the student to make an appointment with a professional counselor we knew, who is also a pilot, for the purpose of addressing the student's phobia about tests. The student was enthusiastic about the idea, because it appeared to be a good plan for overcoming his major career hurdle.

I then explained the situation to the examiner. "If the student wants to be a pilot," I was told, "there's no reason why he shouldn't go for it." As it turned out, I took another position shortly thereafter, and wasn't able to personally finish up with that student, but he went on to complete his CFI certificate and begin moving up the career ladder.

The other extreme case of checkride-itis I've experienced involved a rather unlikely student. A twenty-five year fighter pilot with a foreign military service, this gentleman was a former NATO squadron commander. Upon retiring from service with his own country, he had accepted a flight training position in the U.S., conditional upon earning FAA civilian licenses.

Never before having flown light, piston-engined aircraft, the fellow had had a difficult time transitioning to Cessnas and Pipers, especially when it came to stalls and landings. By the time I began working with him on his CFI, he had overcome many of those hurdles, but was still being challenged by the finer points required to teach such skills. I soon realized that some of his previous instructors had unintentionally done him a great disservice. Given this man's maturity and professional background, his young instructors had apparently been uncomfortable about telling a fighter pilot how to fly Cessnas. Even though he was a highly dedicated and receptive student, he had not been rigorously taught the basics because folks were afraid they might insult him.

We honed his flight instructing skills, and then scheduled his checkride several weeks in advance. As practical test day approached, my student became increasingly nervous and agitated. We flew the day before his scheduled ride, and although apprehensive, he did an excellent job. I was quite comfortable in recommending him. With a less-experienced pilot I might have been concerned about checkride-itis, but after all, this guy was accustomed to 500 mile-per-hour terrain-following missions, at fifty feet above the deck. The least of my checkride concerns was stress.

I heard no more until the next afternoon, when I received a panicked call from the student, followed by a not-so-panicked call from the examiner. It turned out that the student had been so upset about the checkride that he had stayed up the two nights before without sleeping. On the morning of the checkride, he was so tired that he overslept, and therefore was delayed in departing. This is an ex-military officer, remember, and being late for him represented the ultimate affront to both the examiner and his own pride.

After an uneventful flight to the examiner's airport, he had parked in the wrong location and after realizing it, was intercepted by airport security while cutting across a field on foot between ramps. He was escorted to the examiner's office by uniformed officers checking his story.

It should be no surprise to anyone that with a start like this, the checkride turned out to be a disaster. The student was crushed when he returned home with his pink slip. The examiner, however, recognized from the student's background that he should be perfectly capable of passing a flight instructor checkride. It was immediately clear to him that the problem at hand was apprehension of the test, rather than piloting skills or aeronautical knowledge.

"I've got an idea," the examiner told me on the phone, "After you've worked with him some more, let's schedule another checkride. But this time we'll make sure he gets some sleep before coming down."

"How will we do that?" I asked.

"Tell you what," said the examiner, "you and I will set a date for the ride, with a noontime meeting. Arrange to fly down here with your student as part of a lesson, with a stopover for lunch. I'll just happen to be in the airport restaurant at the same time, and having a couple hours free...well you get my drift."

This was certainly one of the more creative checkride scheduling arrangements I have ever experienced; not only did it sound like fun, but there was the distinct possibility that it might work. We made the deal, and set up a date.

My student and I flew several brush-up sessions, after which he stated that he felt ready to give it another shot. On the morning of the scheduled day I learned that I would be unable to go along, due to an unexpected conflict, but we were still able to take advantage of the plan. I arranged a final "polish-up" lesson before the test... I had my student teach me a few landings; then we debriefed. "Great job today!" I said, "When shall I schedule the checkride?"

"Any time," said the student, "I'll be free all through next week."

"How about noon?" I asked.

"Today?!" came the incredulous reply.

"Yep, you're well-rested, the examiner is available, and you're sharp as a tack this morning." Although the student was nervous, he had only an hour or two to worry about his test during the flight down. His meeting with the examiner went smoothly, and he aced the test.

My day was made when he phoned me upon return. "I must tell you," said the ex-fighter pilot, "The flight back was really fun. I'm actually learning to enjoy flying Cessnas!"

I tell these stories not to mourn the failures of those tests, but to brag about the victories of finishing up these two pilots' training. In each case I was deeply discouraged to have recommended students for the practical test, only to have them fail miserably. But that's not what I remember today.

Rather, it's the pleasure of having overcome difficult situations to help my students meet their objectives. I went the extra mile to help them, and those efforts were greatly appreciated by two professional pilots who might otherwise not be flying today. Neat stuff!

Preparing CFIs for the Practical Test

Among the most difficult tests for most applicants to prepare for are CFI checkrides. Along with all the material that must be mastered, and learning to fly and demonstrate maneuvers from the right seat, is the challenge of becoming a good teacher.

In my own experience, I've found one of the greatest challenges for CFI applicants is to organize their thoughts and presentations in a manner appropriate to new students they will be teaching. It's important to begin with broad overview of each topic, and then work one's way into the details.

When an uninitiated CFI student teaches a topic to you, or to the examiner for that matter, he or she generally tends to teach at too advanced a level, to skip all the basic stuff and get right into the details. The reason, of course, is that the student knows that the instructor or examiner already knows this stuff, and is trying to impress with the depth of his or her knowledge.

But the examiner expects the presentation to be geared toward a flight student, not an expert. How can you get your CFI applicants thinking on this level? The answer is ridiculously simple, but almost no one ever does it—have your CFI applicant student-teach some lessons to someone who doesn't already know the stuff! I can assure you it will be an eye-opener for most CFI students and that they will likely perform much better on the CFI oral afterwards.

TEN

Getting Them Back for the Next Rating

Instructors are treated to a special feeling each and every time one of our students passes a checkride. There's pride in the student, pride in ourselves, and sometimes even a bit of relief — to be done with that student and on to the next one.

But many of us have the bad habit of washing our hands of our students after the checkride is over. That's not necessarily a conscious decision, but rather one of letting the student get on with his or her own flying. It's natural to expect that you'll get a call next time the student needs some help.

Calls from former students, however, don't come as frequently as one might expect. One reason is that new private pilots tend to feel that once certificated, they're supposed to know everything. Accordingly they are often uncomfortable about contacting their instructor with questions, or asking for more dual.

Another problem is proficiency. Newly-rated pilots, all too often, do less flying once family and friends have all had their rides. While new pilots sometimes claim that they're tapped out of cash after all those flying lessons, more often the problem is tied to lack of interest from their families, or simply not being creative in planning flying destinations and activities. Regardless of the cause, the effect of doing less flying is always the same: less proficiency and less confidence. As the pilot's newly-won confidence begins to erode, so does the urge to go out and fly.

FIRST AND FOREMOST — KEEP THOSE FORMER STUDENTS FLYING!

So when it comes to repeat business, there's good reason not to allow pilots to remain inactive for too long, if you can help it. For most pilots, confidence about their flying skills seems to erode before their actual competence in flying the plane. In other words, their comfort with flying diminishes well before they lose the skills. If you can just get them up in the air again, they're almost always delighted to find that little brush-up is required to bring them up to speed again.

But the longer they go without flying, the less confident they are in their ability to go back to it. And that means less and less likelihood that they'll go on to earn future ratings.

When your former students quit flying, everyone suffers. The student has invested a good deal of money and time, without harvesting the enjoyment that comes from years of flying. A quitter is certainly not going to pursue any proficiency training or new ratings, nor is it likely that he or she is going to refer many friends for lessons, so both you and your flight school suffer lost business. Finally, the general aviation community suffers through loss of yet another pilot from our dwindling ranks.

What can you and I do to keep former students flying? Half the battle in keeping newly rated pilots flying is continuing that proactive instructing we talked about earlier, even once the certificate is earned.

Continue to Be a Resource, Long After Your Student has Moved On

As part of your after-the-checkride congratulatory speech, make it clear to your newly licensed pilots that your relationship is far from over.

"Call on me any time for advice!" you should tell them, and then spell out the kinds of help you're available to provide. "Got a trip coming up, and you'd like another opinion on a tough weather decision? Phone me! I'll print out a copy of the weather over at my place, and we'll go over it together." It could easily make the difference on whether or not they make that trip.

For your own good and theirs, you owe it to your former students to call them up regularly with questions and encouragement about their flying activities.

"Where've you been flying lately? Any interesting experiences?" Along with their flying stories you're going to hear about their concerns, and probably field a few questions about their latest adventures.

Be sure to raise technical questions which might merit your assistance. "So you're flying to Colorado this summer — exciting! I assume you've done some reading about mountain flying. It's not the same as what we're used to here in Iowa, you know."

Then there are checkout opportunities in different aircraft types. "I gather you're getting into longer cross-country flights these days. Is the ol' 172 still fast enough for you? We could do an Archer check-out in two hours or less. You'll pick up ten knots, plus gain enough additional payload to bring along your mother-in-law. Once you reach 100 hours total time, we've got a number of faster airplanes you might enjoy flying, too."

In each of these cases, there's a tendency for CFIs to be concerned about butting into the flying activities of their now-rated former students. But the fact is that most new pilots don't know what the right questions are, much less the answers. Your friend may well think that flying the Archer requires a commercial certificate, or 5,000 hours. After all, the wing *is* on the bottom!

By following up with your students, you will not only increase the possibility of more flying together, but you'll be doing a real service in enhancing the safety, utility and enjoyment of another pilot.

"You're going out to test-fly twins? Thinking of buying a Baron? Gee, if you'd like another opinion I'd be glad to come along!"

Just as importantly, you're going to quickly learn on your follow-up calls whether or not these pilots have been flying, and if not, why not.

Invite Former Students Along on Interesting Flights

Another really great way to keep your students flying, and to fire them up about more training at the same time, is to invite them along on flights which will expose them to new situations and more advanced aircraft.

Since night training requirements for the private pilot certificate are so limited, new pilots tend to be nervous about flying at night, and only marginally proficient by the time they complete their checkrides. So those folks are ideal prospects to join you for night currency and night cross-country flights.

Need to do some hood work? Invite a former student along to be your safety pilot. It's a great way to introduce him to principles of instrument flight, plus he gets to log time as a "required crew member."

For that matter, invite former students along, whenever you can, for a real IFR trip. Think about it—how many non-instrument rated pilots have ever experienced flight "in the soup"? Most don't even know what instrument flying is all about, and can't imagine what they'd be doing taking instrument lessons. But I can assure you, on their first IFR experience, you'll hold their rapt attention right up to the grand finale of breaking out over the runway at your destination. Instrument flying is such a kick that you may instantly earn yourself a new instrument student, someone who never would have considered it without having been invited along.

The same sort of opportunity exists on flights made in high-performance aircraft. The average new private pilot has done all of his flying in something pretty slow, like a Cessna 152 or a Warrior. As you well know, cross-country flying in those smaller birds can be really slow, especially against a headwind. But traveling in a Skylane, a Bonanza, or a Cessna 210 is a whole new adventure, because of the greater speeds and comfort involved. Remember your first ride in a 182? I remember mine like it was yesterday. Wow! The throaty rumble of those 235 horses was what first inspired me to move up to the big stuff.

Flying even the smallest twin is great adventure for a recently certificated pilot. Obviously, one needs to use a little discretion in turning on former students to the joys of flying a Baron; go for the folks who can afford to buy one!

Finally, be sure to call on your former students to join you for fly-ins and other pleasure trips. They might not elect to do these things on their own, due to lack of confidence or initiative. But by inviting them along you expose new pilots to adventures they'll probably want to repeat in the future.

Before we leave the subject, who pays for these sorts of invite-along flights? Obviously it's difficult to phone someone up, invite them to join you for a cross-country in the Seneca, and then ask for them to rent the plane and pay for your time. The answer, of course, is to split the cost.

When inviting them clarify that, while you'll be happy to put an entry in their logbook, it's not a formal lesson, but rather a flight you'd like to share as you would with any fellow pilot. As you might imagine, it's very important to have this discussion beforehand, differentiating between pleasure flying the two of you split, and formal lessons in the future which they'll have to pay for.

Connect Your Former Students So They'll Fly Together

One approach I have found valuable in keeping my former students flying, is to circulate a list to all of them, including (with permission, of course) a brief paragraph about each, what days they are available to fly, and any particular types of flying they like to do. That way, when one wants to go somewhere with another pilot, he or she can call a few people off that list, and see who's available to join them.

I have found this approach to be particularly valuable with pilots who, for whatever reason, don't seem to enjoy flying alone. Many of these people love to fly, but just never develop the initiative, or perhaps it's the confidence to fly without company.

Not only does putting your ex-students together get them out flying, but it gives them the opportunity to learn from each other, and put their heads together to make weather-related and other challenging decisions.

KEEP IN TOUCH WITH YOUR FORMER STUDENTS—
THEY'LL CALL YOU FOR LESSONS

Keep your name alive with your former students, and they'll come back to you. Give them courtesy calls when flight reviews and medical certificates come due. Set up a mailing list, and use it to advise former students of worthwhile aviation activities in the area. Pass along articles covering issues relevant to their flying, like airspace changes, pertinent Advisory Circulars, and reference cards for weather codes.

One CFI friend of mine sent holiday and birthday cards to all his ex-students. (He surreptitiously lifted birthdates off his students' medicals!) As a result, every few weeks an old student would come in for a flight review, or a referred friend would call about lessons.

OFFER COURSES ON TOPICS OF SPECIAL INTEREST

Among the more obvious teaching opportunities outside of ratings is instruction required for recurrent training or currency. Keep track of when your former students' flight reviews and instrument proficiency checks are due, then contact them in advance to offer your services.

The trick in teaching FRs and IFR checks is to make the training rigorous, so that each student is challenged during the process, and then afterwards feels really great about what was accomplished—the thrill of mastering a tough workout often motivates them to try something new.

The FAA's excellent "Wings" proficiency program (*see* Advisory Circular 61-91) also offers the opportunity to set up a regular course of recurrent training for your pilot acquaintances.

Pilots have this ingrained notion that the only legitimate reason to learn anything is to attain a new certificate or rating. But there's plenty of other aviation know-how that pilots will invest in. Offer special courses addressing piloting topics of local interest. Some courses, like mountain flying, and over-water flying, are well suited to training including both ground school and several hours of flight instruction.

Other courses, such as one on regional weather, offer you the opportunity to meet potential students for future ratings, while enhancing flight safety.

No multi-engine ground school? Start one! It's true that no written is required for the multi-engine rating, but we all know there's plenty of material to be covered there. Hopefully some of those classroom students don't yet have an instructor, and after experiencing your spellbinding teaching style, they'll sign up.

"Advanced" flying seminars can be offered on any number of topics, to get those pilots back out to the airport.

"Pinch-hitter courses" are terrific for teaching spouses and companions about flying—not only do you expose some new folks to flying in the process, but pinch-hitter courses have the effect of improving family support for that primary pilot in the family.

Organize Pleasure Flying Trips

For many of us, what makes a given flying trip really fun is having a mission for the flight. Pilots might "hem and haw" a bit about hopping in the plane to fly around locally just for fun. But when it comes to a real mission, like flying up to the mountains to pick up the kids from summer camp, now *that's* exciting!

These days more and more flight schools are organizing group flights, often in a club format, for their customers. Usually it's set up in the form of a once-per-month group outing, where pilots and their families travel somewhere by plane for activities ranging from dinner to ski weekends.

The pilots pay for all their expenses, of course, including plane rental, but the FBO does the planning for the trip, so it's as easy as just signing up. The planning requires lots of work, on someone's part, and a certain amount of marketing to the pilots is required. But there's hardly a better way to spread enthusiasm about flying than to set up this kind of travel format for pleasure pilots, their friends and families.

Train Students So *Their Passengers* Will Enjoy Flying

Now for one of the most crucial points in keeping your students flying, and returning to you and your flight school in the future. It is absolutely imperative that, as part of your flight training process, you train new pilots to make flying a wonderful experience for their passengers. In many respects, what you need to do is train your students to give "demo flights," in the sense of the introductory lesson covered earlier in this book.

We've talked a little in earlier chapters about how training your students to satisfy their passengers adds to their confidence as pilots. But there's another reason for making those passengers happy. Those other folks play a huge part in determining whether or not your student will be coming back for the next rating. Once a new pilot is hooked, he or she may have no doubts about the value of investing in flying, but spouses and family members are concerned about how that money is spent, too.

In a sense, your training has to sell those other family members on flying. If your newly hatched pilot is lucky, he or she will have several opportunities to introduce friends and family to the joys of the air. And depending on how those flights go, they may choose to fly more with their new pilot, or never to do it again.

Avoid Telling War Stories

Tell your students to avoid telling "war stories" in front of friends and family. One private pilot I know is married to a woman who is petrified of flying, but to her credit she cares so much about her husband that she flies with him anyway. That's a wonder, because this guy makes even the most docile flight sound like the emergency of his life. Every flying story is liberally peppered with phrases like, "I barely maintained control," and "the controls were virtually ripped from my hand by the crosswind."

Most likely this fellow's objective is simply to impress his audience with his masterful flying skills, but the effect over several years of flying has been to drive his family further and further from enjoyment of his favorite hobby, and to scare many of his closest friends away from ever joining him.

That Critical First Flight of a Newly Certificated Pilot

One of the first acts of your newly certificated ex-flight student will be to take his closest friends and family for an airplane ride. This is a day that the proud new pilot has been looking forward to throughout his training, yet most likely his lucky new passengers have been dreading it.

Likely as not, those passengers haven't flown much, if ever, in a light plane. Since that new pilot once dinged the family car, or can't fix a broken sink, or sometimes forgets to turn off the porch light before going to bed, family members sometimes feel that their new aviator can't possibly have what it takes to be a pilot. Besides, they heard all about his travails during training, and since he did earn his certificate only last week, he's obviously a novice.

A smooth first flight gives passengers the confidence they need to believe in their pilot. Accordingly, your student needs to know all the tricks to giving his passengers a wonderful experience, as well as the importance of making it that way.

Tell the new pilot to compare piloting of airplanes to riding motorcycles. Driving a motorcycle is a blast, but riding on the back is a total drag, because the passenger is totally out of control. Point out to your new pilots this comparison: their passengers will have the same reaction to a wild ride on their first airplane flight, as the back-seat rider on a motorcycle.

"It's simple," I tell them, "treat your passengers to wing-overs on their first ride, and your career as family pilot may well be over."

Just as instructors do on an intro flight, new pilots need to introduce their families gently, by flying early in the day, avoiding wind and turbulence, and handling the controls with supreme smoothness.

Your new private pilot just spent fifty or sixty hours mastering flight maneuvers in airplanes, and he or she should be justifiably proud of doing it. But those are *not* the skills to demonstrate on the first flight with the family. It may sound obvious to you, but a surprising number of new pilots try to impress new passengers with their newly-acquired flying skills by performing stalls and steep turns. This can be an extremely expensive mistake, because once family members have become frightened of flying, there's a very good likelihood they won't do it again.

One of my few great regrets as a flight instructor comes from an experience I had shortly after earning my CFI rating.

Several of my close family members are also pilots. One of them, "Bob," was just finishing up graduate school and had not flown for a number of years. With the glow of my new CFI wings shining brightly, I phoned him with a generous offer.

"Hey Bob, I know you haven't flown for a few years, and your birthday's coming up. What do you say about coming down for a visit, and I'll give you a flight review for your present."

An enthusiastic private pilot, Bob was delighted. Only a few weeks later he showed up for his flight review. With him was his new girlfriend, Elaine. There were introductions all around, and the three of us walked out to preflight the airplane.

"Are you a pilot?" I asked Elaine. "No," she replied, "but I've always wanted to go up in a small plane."

"Well," I told her, "While we're doing our maneuvers, why don't you relax over a soda in the pilot lounge. Then, when we get back, Bob can take you up for a ride."

"Oh no," she said, "I want to go along with you guys now."

"We'll be doing some stalls and steep turns, I…."

"Come on!" interrupted Bob, "Elaine won't have any problem. She loves rollercoasters. This'll be nothing for her."

Clearly this was something they both wanted to do.

"Well okay," I said. "Just let us know, Elaine, if you get uncomfortable during the flight and want to come back."

We pre-flighted the plane, buckled everyone in, and cranked 'er up.

Several times during the flight I looked back at Elaine to see how she was doing. Each time she smiled and waved.

Bob did a great job on his first flight review, and upon completing the airwork we cruised back to the airport to do some landings. As we prepared to enter the pattern I turned around to ensure that Elaine had her seat belt secure for landing. Her face was literally green.

Bob squeaked the landing; we taxied back, and Elaine ran into the ladies' room. I was concerned about ruining their day, but Bob shrugged the whole thing off. "She'll be fine in a few minutes." Elaine said the same thing, after re-acclimating to *terra firma*.

There's nothing in this story that most of us haven't experienced a time or two. The hard part for me has been the aftermath. Bob and Elaine continued to date, and eventually went on to get married. That was over fifteen years ago. Bob has not piloted an airplane since we made that flight, because Elaine won't go up in small planes. Until recently she required coaxing even for airline travel.

I'll never know for sure if that flight review was the reason why Bob quit flying, but I've never forgiven myself for the possibility that it could be. Elaine certainly never went up in a light airplane with Bob again. You can bet that I've never taken an inexperienced passenger along on that sort of a training flight again, no matter how strong the coaxing.

Appropriate skills to demonstrate on your first flight with a given passenger are smoothness, professionalism, great takeoffs and landings, and perhaps cross-country ability.

Explain What to Expect in Advance

One mark of a professional pilot that everyone can relate to is the preflight briefing. After all, that's what happens every time a passenger gets on an airliner, isn't it? So along with the regulatory obligations of a pilot to brief passengers before flying, there's also an opportunity to share some additional information which both demonstrates the pilot's know-how, and helps to put passengers at ease.

Prior to cranking up the engine, pilots of first-time passengers should always spend a few moments explaining what's going to happen through the taxi and takeoff experience. For example, every passenger knows the likely meaning of a flashing light or a beeping horn, right? *Emergency!!!*

Assure your student that the eyes of passengers in the back seat will be glued in terror on that little blinking transponder reply light throughout the flight—that is, until the marker beacon captures their attention on final. Pilots need to point out before starting the engine that passengers will probably notice several flashing lights during the flight, and perhaps hear a horn, and that all of it is perfectly normal.

Another very frightening thing for passengers is turbulence. That first ride should never be made on any day when turbulence is likely, nor when the weather looks threatening for any other reason. And since you've taught your students how to recognize indicators of turbulence ahead in flight, encourage them to point it out to passengers before getting there.

"See those hills up there, Barb? Since there's a breeze blowing over them from the west, we may experience a few bumps 'til we get to the other side." If turbulence does exist over those hills, the passengers know what to expect, so the experience will be less traumatic. And if there's no turbulence... well, they'll be impressed by their knowledgeable pilot all the same.

Where to Fly on the First Flight

Don't take your spouse up to "fly around for an hour," on his or her first flight, but rather go to a destination your passenger would love to visit, ideally one where the advantages of going by air are obvious.

Too many pilots think that, since they love flying, their friends and families will, too. If only life were that simple. Those of us who've been flying for long know well of the many family members not interested in traveling with their spouses. So the trick is to use flying as an avenue for doing something family members enjoy, rather than trying to get them to love the flying itself.

Take your girlfriend to lunch. Meet her folks for breakfast. Take her shopping, or boating. In short, fly somewhere in an hour that takes four hours to drive. But take her somewhere that's a special experience made possible by flying.

In my own case, I was already a pilot when I met my wife-to-be. She was willing to put up with a certain amount of flying because it came with the territory, but was not particularly interested in doing it on a regular basis. The breakthrough came when I suggested one weekend that we fly up to visit her folks.

An easy hour-and-a-half flight saved four and a half hours of driving through metropolitan Chicago, making it possible for us to leave after work on Friday, be there for dinner, and then be home for lunch on Sunday. More importantly, my wife quickly realized that I'd gladly tolerate an otherwise-deadly weekend at the in-laws, if I got to fly there. It proved to be one of the best deals we've ever made. In fact, she learned to repeat it very skillfully:

"Want to go to Mom and Pop's next weekend?"

"Well, er...I was planning on, er, cleaning out the garage."

"We could *fly* up on Saturday morning, see my folks for dinner, and then *fly* back after brunch on Sunday."

Any pilot can easily guess who won that discussion every time.

Don't Make the First Flight Too Ambitious

Equally important is that none of those first few flights with the family are *too* ambitious. One fellow I know decided to make his first flying trip after earning his private pilot certificate something to remember, which he undoubtedly succeeded in doing.

Having learned to fly in the Phoenix area, he decided to fly a Cherokee with three close friends to a small airport in Southern Utah to attend a family reunion. This was an ideal use for a light airplane, except it meant a trip of several hundred miles over mountainous terrain in the heat of the summer, with relatively limited fuel reserves.

He did his preflight homework thoroughly prior to departure, including selection of several good alternate airports along the way, and making density altitude calculations so he would not over-fuel at his high-elevation point of departure for the return trip.

The first mistake he made was departing mid-morning. In the heat of Southwest summers, pilots "in the know" make their flights early in the morning, because afternoon turbulence can vary from continuous moderate to occasional severe. But this pilot didn't want to inconvenience his passengers with an "o-dark-thirty" departure on their first flight.

He loaded his three first-time passengers into the plane and they took off. Just over the Utah border, the pilot became uncertain of his position and deviated off course, which as you know is usually a mistake. The more he looked for landmarks the more lost he became, finally deciding to divert to an alternate airport along the way. By this time the air had become turbulent, and his passengers were buried in sick-sacks, adding to the excitement.

By the time he found a suitable airport and landed, he was overdue for the ETA on his VFR flight plan, so Flight Service was looking for the plane over a two-state area. After landing and getting his bearings, the pilot regrouped, refueled, and proceeded with his passengers to their destination.

Although he made some mistakes, this pilot actually did an excellent job of completing a very challenging first flight as pilot-in-command with passengers. The safety of the flight was never compromised, and his thorough preflight planning made getting lost no more than a nuisance. It's just that this was a poor choice for a first flight with passengers new to light planes. Probably the only thing that got his friends to fly with him again was the return trip the next day — there was absolutely no other way to get back home, and that flight proved to be uneventful and smooth as glass.

ELEVEN

The Business of Flight Instructing

For most pilots, flight instructing is the first professional, paid flight position they will hold. While this book is not intended to deliver any sort of legal or tax advice, this is a good place to address some of the important business implications of working as a CFI which are important to understand before going to work.

Any instructor who is not already intimately familiar with such issues as taxes, insurance, and the Federal Regulations as they pertain to flight training, should most certainly make the effort to learn about them before hopping into the airplane with that first student.

CHARGING FOR YOUR SERVICES

Okay, now for the hard part. For some reason, we instructors feel guilty about charging students for our services. There may be any number of reasons for this (perhaps consultation with a psychologist is in order), but it really does seem to be a big problem. First, most of us being impoverished, it's hard to imagine that other people may actually have enough money to pay for flying, so we all-too-often set our rates too low.

Secondly, we seem to have some deep-seated problem about having our students invest in anything besides rental of the airplane. As a result, we undercharge, or worse yet, don't charge at all for instructional time given on the ground.

Consider this: For a student pilot, the plane is worthless without an instructor. Good flight training results exclusively from quality instruction, and if you feel good enough about your skills to teach someone to fly an airplane, then you're certainly entitled to be paid for your time.

I personally experienced a real eye-opener not long ago. I had recently finished teaching a neighbor to fly. He was enthused about flying, and to my amazement, also felt I had done a great job of instructing. He called me several weeks after earning his private certificate, and told me he had a client who was interested in an introductory flying lesson. This man was well-to-do, he told me, and was interested in ultimately buying his own plane.

My neighbor then flattered me by explaining all the nice things he had told his client about me—of my many years of flight instructing, my experience as a commercial pilot in large aircraft, and how I knew so much about flying that I had actually written some books on the subject.

After that introduction, how could I turn him down? I arranged to pick up the prospective student at his house, since he lived nearby, and when I arrived I couldn't help but notice the late-model Mercedes sports car parked in his driveway. We proceeded to the airport, where I encouraged him to do a one-hour first lesson, rather than the short introductory flight my neighbor had recommended.

We walked out onto the ramp to look at the airplanes available for training, and he immediately ruled out the two-seat trainers, settling on a sharp-looking 172 instead. We made our flight, had a pleasant lesson, and took time to see a few sights not too far from the airport.

Afterwards we talked about the process of earning a pilot certificate, what he would be able to do with it, and what sorts of planes he might want to consider buying after earning his certificate.

The bombshell dropped when time came to pay the bill. "How much do I owe?" he asked. The person at the desk calculated the amount, and handed him a bill for $79. The fellow took out his wallet and paid in cash. Then, as we walked out the door he turned to me and asked, "And how much do I owe you?"

"Oh, my fee was included in the bill," I replied.

"You mean the bill for the plane?" His expression changed from a pleasant smile to one of marked irritation. "Why you must not make anything on this stuff!"

He had been convinced he was taking a flying lesson from a true industry expert, and had fully expected to pay real money for it. Learning how little he was to pay had tremendously lowered his opinion of me, since he had assumed up until that point that I was an especially "valuable" instructor. And I had even gone so far as "doing him a favor," by not charging him for ground time.

I will not forget that experience. It caused me to think back over years of instructing, only to realize that not once had anyone ever told me I was charging too much, nor requested a break on ground instruction time.

The moral to this story is painfully simple, and I hope you learn it more quickly than I did. As a flight instructor, you are indeed a professional pilot, and people fully expect to pay for it. Accept that value inherent in your services, do a thorough, caring and professional job, and charge accordingly. You'll make more money and so will your flight school. Perhaps most importantly, your students will respect you for it.

KEEP YOUR RECEIPTS

The moment you begin earning money as a flight instructor, be it full-time, freelance, or as a second job, you begin a relationship with that notorious tax collecting body, the IRS (U.S. Internal Revenue Service). Although flying may seem like too much fun to be officially considered work, you'll still have to declare your income and pay taxes on it. But the good news is that most flight instructors find themselves in a position to deduct many costs of doing business—providing they know how to do it, that is.

Therefore, one of your first acts as a new flight instructor should be a meeting with your accountant or bookkeeper. At flight instructor wages, you may think you can't afford to invest in such a meeting. But if you do any volume of business, the cost will be paid back to you many times over, through enhanced income and saved taxes.

Active flight instructors often find themselves able to deduct a wide range of expenses from their taxes, resulting in savings equal to one third or more of qualifying expenditures. How about saving $100 on your new $300 headset? Not only is equipment such as headsets and flight cases often deductible, but also charts and other supplies, non-reimbursed recurrent training expenses, your flight physical, and in some cases, the cost of adding additional flight instructor ratings. Promotional expenses like advertising, printing, and long distance phone calls are usually deductible, too.

A good accountant or bookkeeper can tell you ahead of time what kinds of expenses might be deductible for you, based on factors such as other sources of income, and whether you are self-employed or work for a flight school. You'll learn what records must be kept in order to qualify for those deductions, how taxes will be calculated, and any special considerations for filing. Self-employed flight instructors can also benefit by asking for help in planning issues, like budgeting for their business, and setting instructional rates.

In many cases there is no charge for this sort of "exploratory" meeting, because the accountant or bookkeeper hopes to win you as a regular tax preparation client. When there is a fee, control the cost by clarifying the purpose and duration of the meeting in advance. In this case, explain ahead of time your objectives for the meeting, ask how much time will be required to cover them, whether there will be a fee, and if so how much. By agreeing on all this ahead of time, you can arrange to buy however much of your accountant's time might be required, be it a half hour or an hour, without getting into an unknown or open-ended billing arrangement.

For those too cheap or too busy to meet with a financial professional before getting started with their instructing, I can tell you up front that a big part of tax record-keeping involves keeping receipts. Ask for and keep every receipt that might even remotely relate to your professional flying activities. That way you'll at least have a chance of putting together those deductions later. Just keep in mind that an investment of forty or fifty bucks to meet with an accountant now, may save you hundreds or even thousands of dollars later!

COMPLY WITH THE REGULATIONS

New instructors are often so excited about finally getting paid to fly, that they don't pay much attention to the details of the regulations affecting them. Along with the obvious stuff, like the need to keep flight instructor records as per the regulations, there are other less obvious impacts of the regulations which, if ignored, can come back to haunt unfortunate violators later in their careers.

First and foremost, remember that when instructing you will almost always be pilot-in-command. As a result, any violation regarding airplane airworthiness will likely fall on your shoulders. Make it your business to know for sure when the various aircraft you use are or are not legally airworthy, and avoid flying them when in doubt.

Secondly, be sure to understand and conform to any flight and duty time restrictions which may apply to your activities. Instructors are notorious for flying as many hours as are humanly possible in a day, and then some. Be careful, it's all too easy to break the regulations by flying more than the legal limit in a twenty-four hour period. This issue becomes especially complicated for CFIs mixing their instructional activities with flight duties in the charter department.

Of course, it's imperative that you and your students comply with all regulations pertaining to the flying itself. If your student violates Class B Airspace, there's a very high likelihood that you, as instructor, will be "called onto the carpet" along with your student.

Aviation Safety Reporting System

Along this same line, be sure that you and your soloing students understand the benefits, limitations, and procedure for filing ASRS (Aviation Safety Reporting System) reports with NASA (National Air and Space Administration). Get a copy of the current Advisory Circular and study it! As of time of writing, timely filing of ASRS reports (sometimes known as NASA reports) by pilots who may have violated a regulation, can often result in avoiding FAA penalties if the violation is found to have occurred. It's worth your while as an instructor to understand use of these reports, and pass that knowledge on to your students. Be sure to carry a few blank ASRS report forms in your flight case, where they're accessible if you need them.

CARRY ADEQUATE INSURANCE

Liability and insurance are two interrelated topics that most pilots prefer to ignore. While burying your head may feel better, these are in fact subjects that must be addressed head-on. The term *liability* refers to the issue of who's at fault if something goes wrong. Until becoming an instructor, your liability as a pilot was basically limited to your own flying mistakes. But for an instructor there's additional liability associated with the flying of your students. If your student mistakes a city bus for the runway on his first solo, who will pay for the crushed hats? (Cross your fingers that the heads supporting them are uninjured.) Will the student join those bus passengers in suing you, claiming poor flight training was the cause of the accident?

While it's obvious that doing a good job of flight training is important in preventing accidents, it's impossible to avoid all potential for errors and accidents. That's why instructors must carry insurance.

How much insurance? And what kind? You'll need to meet with a professional on this topic, too. The meeting itself won't cost you anything, but odds are you'll have to invest in some additional coverage when you begin instructing. The first step is to do some information-gathering at the place where you instruct.

Your flight school, or other owner or operator of the airplanes you fly, likely carries some sort of insurance already. Not surprisingly, that insurance almost certainly protects her or him with liability coverage, along with some "hull coverage" to pay for damage sustained by the airplane. But how well are you covered when flying or instructing in a given airplane? And to what extent?

The answer can vary tremendously, depending on whose plane you're flying, but odds are that your own liability, should an accident occur, is not well protected. In addition, there's a very good chance that you could be liable to pay for expensive damages to the plane itself. This is because the hull coverage carried by many aircraft operators tends to have high deductibles, in order to keep insurance rates down. As a result, you (or your student) could easily be obligated to pay $500 to $1,000 or more to cover the deductible for damage to an airplane.

So collect all the information you can from your employer or other operator regarding current insurance coverage on the airplanes you fly. (A copy of the insurance policy is best.) Then meet or talk with a reputable aircraft insurance professional to determine what, if any additional insurance may be required to protect you as an instructor. A good place to begin the process is with your favorite pilot organization.

AOPA, NAFI, and EAA generally offer discount insurance policies to their members. Unless you own your own airplane, your most likely fit as an instructor will be under the category of "renter's insurance." Personal coverage could well set you back $75 to $150 per year, but can you afford to do without it? The fact is that insurance, like your headset and your charts, is part of the cost of working as a professional. Been over to your accountant yet? Uncle Sam will probably help pay for your business insurance; it's tax deductible!

TWELVE

The Flight School—Framework for Success

Until now, our discussion has primarily addressed the individual flight instructor, with little direct reference to the flight school he or she likely works for. This is because one major objective of this book is to empower CFIs to effectively promote flight training even with little support from others.

Yet it should be obvious that the most effective recruiting occurs when flight schools and their CFIs team up, each supporting the efforts of the other to spread the word to potential pilots, start them flying, and then keep them at it. This chapter is designed to guide both flight school managers and individual CFIs towards building an effective team approach for attracting and retaining customers.

Perhaps the best way to consider the relationship between flight school and instructor from a customer's point of view, is to compare flight students with consumers of health care services.

Patients seeking medical care often go to great lengths searching out a reputable clinic or hospital for treatment. Yet, once there, they must respect and trust the individual doctor treating them or they'll leave, no matter how reputable the clinic may be. On the other hand, even the best doctors in solo practice lack the customer-drawing power of their peers who work for well-known clinics.

It's the same with flight training. Ideally, the reputation, image, and structure of the flight training company provide a framework of professionalism for the CFIs who work there, while each individual instructor represents the company in delivering service to the customer. That's why sharp instructors teamed up with a reputable company present a powerful business combination.

LAYING THE GROUNDWORK

Since public perception is so important in attracting customers, what do prospects look for in a flight school? A solid training organization needs to project the same sort of image that customers expect when making a large investment in any service: an established company delivering good service, a quality program, oversight of the training process, and lasting support for future flying activities.

Meeting these customer expectations is very important because we want each prospect walking in the door to think, "this is a great place!" rather than "I don't feel good about this, but maybe they can talk me into it." Then, if the company is as good as customers expect it to be, signing them up is a relatively easy matter.

First Impressions

The latest industry recruiting initiatives are designed to target the sort of affluent pleasure flier who sustained general aviation during the golden era of the seventies. These folks are enthusiastic and they can afford to fly, but it will take increasing sophistication of our facilities, equipment and customer service to sell them.

By now you've probably heard the industry thinking on your competition. When it comes to recreational flying, it's not the FBO across the field competing for the dollars of your prospective students, but rather all of the other recreational activities they have to choose from.

This means that you should be measuring the cachet of your flight training business against luxury car dealers, boat, motorcycle, and snowmobile showrooms, country clubs and ski shops, rather than the flight school across the way. We in the flight training business need to be visiting those places, and learning everything we can about our competition. It's unlikely that the luxury car dealers down the road view you as competition, so don't hesitate to make a few appointments with the managers of places you admire, and ask for some advice.

Customers Must Feel Welcome at Your Facility

One of my nuttier friends in the flight training business delights in traveling around by car, trying to find the offices of his competitors at nearby airports.

"When you *fly* into an airport," he says, "there are signs all over the ramp telling you where to find everything."

"But try driving to the airport, as most new-pilot customers would. It's almost impossible to find most flight schools. And if you *are* lucky enough to find the building, good luck figuring out how to get inside!"

While moving your facility to a better location may not be feasible, installing effective signage certainly is. Not only must your prospective customers be guided from the nearest major thoroughfare all the way to your building, but from the parking area there must be an obvious entrance which *invites the public inside.*

Most people (other than burglars) are extremely uncomfortable about entering what seems like a back door or one "for employees only," yet that is exactly how many flight school entrances appear. Each small increment of discomfort introduced to a visiting prospect decreases the likelihood that you'll see that person again.

If you can afford no other improvements on the building which houses your business, be sure that the entryway and customer reception area convey to anyone driving up, "We're glad to see you; come on in!"

Condition of Your Aircraft

There's a pretty fair chance that prospective customers arriving at the flight school came to you directly from the comfort of luxurious leather and digital cockpits — in their cars! What will they think upon first encounter with your airplanes?

Americans are used to being owners, not renters, and most pilot prospects entertain at least the dream of one day owning their own planes. The average non-pilot believes that planes are more luxurious and more high-tech than cars; at least, that's what they've seen on TV. This gives us some idea of how prospective pilots envision the planes they plan to own — some sort of hybrid progeny of the Space Shuttle, a Ferrari, and a Manhattan penthouse.

The only reason we have a chance to meet those perceptions is that most prospects already know they'll have to learn in a rental plane, so it's reasonable to assume that their expectations have been lowered few notches, say, to the level of a nice rental car with wings. (In aviation terms that might correspond loosely to a loaded top-of-the-line Bonanza.)

Obviously, each of us is limited to what we have available in our training fleets, but it's easy to see what a potentially huge gap there is between customer expectations and even the nicest rental trainer. That's why it's so critically important to keep our training aircraft in the nicest condition possible.

When you rent a car how do you decide whether to use that car rental company again in the future? Price is probably only a small factor, the bigger factors being customer service and the condition of the car.

How did you feel last time you rented a filthy car, or one with torn seats? Ever found a pop can in the glove compartment? Or had your luggage ruined by a leaky oil container in the back seat? I suspect that this has rarely happened to you, but if it did, you certainly didn't go back to that company for your next rental.

Most rental cars are well cleaned between customers, for several reasons. First, it makes the customers more comfortable, because they figure that cars which look clean and sharp on the outside, are probably in tip-top shape mechanically, too. Secondly, companies can charge more for cars when customers expect that they'll be clean and fresh. Most importantly, spotless rental vehicles are what it takes to compete.

So if anyone on your staff forgets what a nice rental vehicle must look like to keep those customers coming back, just send them down to the nearest rental car clean-up lot for a few hours. That's what *we* are competing against.

Opportunity Starts With a Phone Call

For an eye-opening example of what needs to be done for our industry to compete, it's not even necessary to leave the office. Just pick up the phone and make a few calls to flight schools in your area. Ask the person who answers at each school for information regarding introductory flights and flying lessons, and then listen carefully to the answers. (Have a friend phone your own flight school, and ask the same questions.) Here are the comments of one instructor who recently made such calls in her local area:

"Dear Greg,

I had an interesting experience about a week ago that might interest you. I thought I would just do a little local market research. So I phoned about ten FBOs to see how they handled a basic inquiry call—'How much is an introductory flight?' The responses (except for one) astonished me.

The people answering the phone were friendly but they had no clue how to present value and benefits (no one identified themselves as a flight instructor). A typical response was an immediate price quote without an explanation of what I would receive; i.e. 'Well the 150 is $39 and the 172 is $49' (assuming I knew what those numbers meant, or cared). I always had to ask, 'Well what do I get?'

Answers were very vague. For example, 'Well you get to do almost everything—you know, preflight the airplane and then takeoff for about 30 minutes and fly around and stuff…Then you'll come down and talk about it and stuff.'

Another went into great detail about two confusing programs, one of which would save me 10% on 'stuff.' (I've never heard the word *stuff* so often.) So I asked what she meant by 'stuff.' She said, 'like rental, instruction, supplies, and if you 'ding' the plane you won't have to pay the insurance.' (Greg, I'm not kidding you.)

No one asked me my name; no one asked any type of open-ended question to qualify my level of interest or involve me, and *only one* asked if they could send me more information.

I have to say I was absolutely stunned. I'm sure it can't be this bad everywhere. I'm sure the bigger population FBOs are much better, but doesn't it make you wonder...?"

Unfortunately, every CFI reading this knows such problems aren't unique to the above instructor's geographic area. Yet how many flight customers does the average flight school effectively turn away by mishandling telephone inquiries?

Along with a cordial answer, every potential flight training customer expects and deserves a fulfilling experience, beginning with their first telephone call. The only way to ensure this happens is to prepare ahead of time written guidelines for handling such calls, and teach employees to use them. Another approach is to assign a specifically prepared individual to accept every flight training inquiry that comes in.

Customer Service: The Heart of Our Business

What we are talking about, of course, is "customer service," and answering the phone is just the tip of the iceberg.

While development of a comprehensive, quality-oriented customer service program is beyond the scope of this book, that issue simply must be addressed by any flight training enterprise planning to compete and win in today's business environment. Some of us who have been in the business for a long time have become immune to the customer service apathy which traditionally plagues many flight departments. But gone are the days when our businesses can survive having first-time visitors greeted gruffly, or ignored upon their entrance.

Unlike the post office, people do not have to visit our facilities, so anything short of a warm welcome is deadly for business. As one instructor friend aptly put it, "Prospective students shouldn't feel as if they're boarding a sinking ship!"

As it turns out, customer service in the flight training business needs to be more than competent; it must be exceptional. After all, our customers, whether pleasure pilots or aspiring pros, are looking to aviation for adventure and excitement. So they expect to meet upbeat, happy individuals working at the airport.

A good way to kick off your customer service training is with some of the excellent training videotapes and seminars available through industry organizations. For example, AOPA's terrific video with Ralph Hood, "Successful Strategies to Attract and Retain New Students," should be required viewing for every CFI you hire. In a concise and entertaining manner, Mr. Hood lays out a specific and practical dialog for dealing with prospective students, from answering the first customer telephone call, through the initial meeting and introductory lesson; concluding with how to schedule a follow-up lesson before the customer leaves.

NATA offers an equally effective video for introducing line service personnel to customer service concepts, along with (at time of writing) a series of excellent management seminars on the topic for both flight training and line service departments. Obviously offerings like these change all the time, so be alert to the introduction of new courses and educational materials from both aviation organizations and elsewhere.

For first-hand experience of customer-service leaders in our own industry, visit a few recent winners of the annual *Professional Pilot* magazine FBO Contest. These places are selected each year by corporate pilot ballot, and they literally roll out the red carpet for their patrons. Be sure to check out those winning FBOs when you're in their neighborhood.

It has never been more important that every flight school employee, from receptionist to instructor and manager to mechanic, greet each arriving customer with warmth, enthusiasm, and a genuine commitment to making the customer's experience a terrific one.

YOUR CFIs AS A SALES FORCE

Now that we've done what we can to impress prospective customers arriving at the flight school, let's move on to the roles of CFIs in attracting and retaining students.

There's a certain amount of controversy among flight schools as to whether flight instructors should be trained in sales techniques, or not. Some experts feel that CFIs make the best new-pilot salespeople, since they are the ones who deliver the service. The Aircraft Owners and Pilots Association, for example, has identified flight instructors as the key players in attracting new student starts, and backed up that position with a series of instructor incentive programs.

Others feel just as strongly that CFIs should be kept free of sales duties so they can concentrate on their primary mission of teaching. Certainly anyone would agree that business shouldn't interfere with the professional role of the CFI.

Both of these attitudes about CFI sales training are obviously valid, so the direction individual companies should take in this regard varies with the needs and philosophy of each particular flight school.

But regardless of any one flight school's position on formal sales training for flight instructors, there is a legitimate and vital role for CFIs in generating and retaining business. At issue is not so much whether they need to be trained, but rather *how* they need to be trained.

When people talk traditional sales training, there are really only two specific areas of this very broad discipline that make most of us quake with fear. The first is "cold calling," which refers to activities like interrupting naps by knocking on doors and disturbing dinners by randomly telephoning people out of the phone book. The second is "closing," which generally refers to asking for people's money, and collecting signatures on dotted lines.

Relatively few people are naturally equipped with either the skills or confidence required to effectively make cold-calls and close sales; that's why only a limited number of CFIs are well-suited to do full-fledged sales.

But flight schools have the good fortune to be blessed with a group of employees who, if properly encouraged and supported, can most certainly enhance sales, even though that may not be their primary responsibility. CFIs are already educated about the process, requirements, and costs associated with flight training. Since instructors are both aviation enthusiasts and also the major customer contact people for your business, they are in fact ideally suited to fill some very important *sales support* roles at any flight school.

First, your CFIs can do an excellent job of increasing the visibility of your flight school in the community.

Secondly, they can attract potential students to the airport through personal networking methods, as discussed throughout this book.

And finally, flight instructors are indispensable for satisfying and thereby retaining the customers you already have.

Enhancing Business Visibility Through Your Instructors

Flight school businesses are selling a relatively expensive product, and as such need to present flying as a good value. If your people present as professionals, it makes the pricing appear in line with a professional service.

Uniforms should be worn at work to convey professionalism to your customers, and to establish the company's identity. Exactly what these uniforms should be is a matter of personal taste for each flight school's management, but regardless of whether it's white shirts with ties and epaulets, or polo shirts and dress shorts, it's critically important that everyone look clean and natty.

Equally important is what your staff wears *away* from work. As detailed in Chapter 3, to attract new students your flight instructors must be active and visible in the community—and be identifiable as pilots while they are out there. If you think about it, we're incredibly fortunate to be in a business where people have such love for what they do. While normal people want to get away from their jobs during time off, pilots never seem to get tired of talking flying. We want prospective pilots to approach flight instructors in the places where they hang out after work, like at softball games, around the pool, the gym, at restaurants and parties. When instructors wear flying-related clothing, others constantly approach them to talk about it.

Obviously one can't tell employees what to wear on days off, so the trick here is to offer some neat casual apparel they'll *want* to sport off the job. Ask your instructors about what sorts of flying regalia they'd enjoy wearing when away from the office. T-shirts, hats, sweatshirts, lapel pins and the like are useful and inexpensive advertising for any flight school. You might also want to look into items like watches, ties, and jewelry. All of these items can be ordered sporting the flight school logo, in small quantities and at reasonable prices.

Since the whole point is to have your staff wear clothing that promotes aviation, it must be made available at affordable prices. One option is to offer apparel at cost to employees, then sell them at retail in your pilot shop. Wearable items also make great incentive items. Award them to individual employees for special accomplishments, or to the whole staff for achieving sales or performance goals.

Community Involvement

Now that we've got the staff *looking* like pilots, the next trick is to take advantage of their enthusiasm to increase the flight school's visibility in the community. We talked a lot in Chapter 3 about networking opportunities in the community. Flight schools are in a position to tremendously encourage these activities, and increase community awareness in the process.

Host meetings at the airport for community groups like the chamber of commerce, county medical society, professional organizations, and business groups. Invest in booths and exhibits at local airshows and other community events. Support or start local aviation clubs. Who's going to represent you at all these functions?

Your CFIs, of course. Have them wear those terrific uniforms you've developed, and make clear to them that the objective is to recruit new students. When not flying, your instructors need to be out and about, where they'll be seen and recognized as representatives of your flight school. In this respect, part-time instructors can prove to be as valuable as full-timers, because they are likely working other jobs, or otherwise spending more time out in the community.

Your CFIs can do an excellent job of increasing the visibility of your flight school and attracting potential students to the airport; you just need to provide them with the opportunities.

Wonderful Business Cards: You've Got to Have Them

As discussed in Chapter 3, customers purchasing professional services expect quality business cards and printed materials which explain, qualify, and give credibility to their bearers. Quality materials make customers more comfortable about investing their hard-earned money on a service, especially in businesses like ours where there are no hard goods to judge such as boats, ski equipment, and other products with which we compete.

Furthermore, you simply must consider using four-color (full-color) business cards because *our mission is selling adventure.* There are few things as beautiful as an airplane in flight, and we need to capitalize on that.

You probably already know that offset printing of color business cards can be very expensive, given a staff of multiple instructors, if each CFI's cards are ordered separately. The trick for saving money is to order printing of the four-color cards in sheets, which are then saved for imprinting of individual names later. Business cards are not printed one-at-a-time, but rather are produced in multiples on large sheets of card stock, which are then cut into individual cards after printing.

Work with your graphic designer or printer to design some full-color business cards appropriate for adding individual instructor names later. Then have a large quantity of the cards printed (to keep the cost per card down) *minus the names.*

Have your printer or designer save the *uncut* sheets (sometimes called "shells," "masters," or "blanks") in a secure place. Whenever new business cards are needed, any printer can run a few of the already-printed color card sheets through a simple press to add the new names in black, then cut them into cards. Thus you can print small quantities of full-color cards personalized with each instructor's name, at a per-card cost not much higher than a traditional one-color versions.

It's also worthwhile to print some professional-looking full-color postcards and note cards, emblazoned with the flight school name, for use by your staff as thank-you notes and for casual follow-up. (These will be useful not only in the flight training department, but also for maintenance, avionics, and sales customers.) It's perfectly appropriate to use the same photograph for these as on the business cards. Through the right sources, you can get custom postcards for prices as low as $95 for five hundred.

Incidentally, professional photographs for such uses can often be obtained at no charge through the sales or public relations departments of your favorite major aircraft manufacturer.

Team Selling: Set 'em Up and Knock 'em Down

Okay, so we're agreed that flight instructors can increase the visibility of your business, plus attract potential customers to the airport. But that brings us back to the nagging CFI-as-salesperson problem. Once potential customers are invited to the airport, then what?

One of the biggest objections to using CFIs as a sales force is that "pilots are poor business people. They are interested only in flying airplanes." Of course it's hard to go along with such a gross generalization, but at the same time it does make sense that not every flight instructor is cut out for selling $4,000 flight training packages.

But instructors can do a great deal to attract new business, without having to actually make the final sale. It's long-standing practice when selling big-ticket items that two individuals are often involved in the sales process; one does the prospecting, while the other does the closing. In the case of flight schools, the trick is to support and encourage CFIs to spread the word and invite prospects to the airport, while assigning someone else on staff responsibility to "close" the sale.

The individual doing the selling can be the flight school owner, the flight training manager, the marketing manager, or anyone else with demonstrated sales aptitude. But each new prospective customer should be steered to this in-house expert, who then assesses the prospect's needs, recommends a plan of action, and hopefully, signs up a new flight training customer.

It works like this: Flight instructors (and any other flight school employees, for that matter) are encouraged to invite prospective pilots to the airport, without obligation to "sell" anything. The reason might be for an introductory lesson, a tour of the facility, or just to look at the airplanes.

Once they're at the flight school, the CFI introduces prospective students to the designated sales expert, "Bill, I'd like you to meet Rhea Lexpert, our flight training manager. I know you had a few questions about the process for earning a pilot certificate, and the costs of doing it. Rhea is the expert on the subject; she'll be able to answer all of your questions."

This "set 'em up and knock 'em down" team selling approach allows CFIs to qualify prospects and invite them out to the airport, where the assigned manager or salesperson then "closes" the deal and signs up the customer.

Your Flight Training Customers as a Sales Force

Now that we've addressed flight instructors as a sales force, let's expand that army of general aviation promoters to include your business's flight students and other pilot customers. Sounds mercenary, but it's not.

Let's face it, most pilots love flying so much that they make great aviation evangelists. And new pilots are among the most enthusiastic in every aviation community. Make flying a great experience for them, and they'll trumpet the news all over town and beyond.

We've already addressed some of the techniques for helping these folks enjoy the training process. "Retention" we've called it up until now, but perhaps a better word is "empowerment."

Make your flight students proud to be pilots, and they will in turn introduce their friends and associates to aviation, to the great place where they learned to fly, and to that special instructor who taught them.

What can the flight school do to promote this? We've already talked about the need to deliver quality training, and the need to "nip in the bud" the students' technical, motivational, and confidence problems.

But there's more. Present your flight students with awards for their milestone flying achievements like first solo, long solo cross-country, and earning of certificates and ratings. Every award you dispense to a flight customer for any accomplishment should be selected with two specific objectives in mind: first, to honor and excite the customer, and secondly, to spread their enthusiasm about flying among their friends and relatives.

This means that if you're going to present a solo certificate, it should be really cool, and awarded to the student in a frame. We're not talking big money, here; attractive picture frames are very inexpensive at the local discount store. And consider the return: an unframed certificate goes in a drawer at home, while a framed one is proudly displayed in your flight customer's office at work, or in the den at home.

For just a few variations on this approach, one flight school I talked to orders trophies from the local trophy shop to award at solo. Another frames the traditional solo shirttail together with a certificate and a hand-drawn cartoon, and yet another takes a photo at solo, and mounts it on a framed certificate. Flying-related posters and office desk items are also great award items, for the same reasons.

As with your instructors, whenever possible award your flight students with nifty flying stuff they can wear (emblazoned tastefully with your flight school logo, of course). Your students are proud of their flying, and apparel like T-shirts, sweatshirts, neckties, and jewelry lets everyone know that they're pilots. (Hopefully their friends will be inspired to come out for lessons soon, too.)

One flight school manager told me about special hats he issues only upon first solo. "Students approach me all the time," he said, "asking, 'When do I get my hat?' Can you believe it? They're investing $4,000 so they can get a hat!"

Another important aspect of rewarding accomplishments is to do it in front of others, with a bit of ceremony. Couples know all about this—flowers for someone you care about must always be sent to work, not home. That's because what makes the act really special is having others see it! Handing a solo certificate to a flight customer in the hallway near the restroom, or outside in the parking lot, just doesn't cut it. The better approach is to hold a weekly or monthly coffee-and-cookies reception to present them.

Equally important is to make public your students' personal flying accomplishments by sending news releases to local and regional newspapers. Whenever possible, include a photograph of the student, shown in front of an airplane, or in the cockpit. (For more detail on effective news releases, see Chapter 3.)

Many flight schools offer incentives to their customers for making referrals. Again, it's best to make these incentives something that increase your visibility, or indirectly inspire more business in one way or another. Incentives are often most effective when they are tied to a student accomplishment, or presented in a friendly, rather than institutional manner.

One flight school manager recently told me of an interesting incentive program used in his flight school's private pilot program. Each student earns special coupons upon reaching each of three key milestones during training. Upon completion of first solo, and then again at first cross-country solo and upon earning the private pilot certificate, each training customer is awarded free introductory lesson certificates to be given away as gifts to friends and family. This clever approach capitalizes on student enthusiasm at the high points of training to sell flying to others they think will enjoy it.

Student Retention: Perhaps Our Biggest Business Opportunity

Where does new business come from anyway? And how do we know if we're targeting the right customers? These are incredibly difficult questions for which there are no easy answers, but one thing that's for certain is bringing in new customers is very costly.

Attracting new flight students is expensive because it's so hard to ferret them out from the masses of the general public. Since the total number of potential flight customers is fairly small, and our prospects are scattered over a wide variety of occupations and interests, we need to expose a large number of people to our offerings in order to attract the relatively small percentage who are interested in learning to fly.

And since marketing to a large public audience requires expensive methods such as large-scale advertising and direct mail campaigns, attracting new customers in that manner can be uneconomical. It would be a cata-strophic situation for many flight schools, if every bit of new business had to indeed come from new customers. (This also explains why starting a new flight school can be so challenging.)

The key point is the need to differentiate *new business* from *new customers*. Among sales types in almost every industry there's an oft-quoted maxim called "the 80/20 rule," which states that *80% of new business comes from existing customers*, while only 20% of new business comes from new customers.

The implications of the 80/20 rule to flight training businesses are important ones. First, there's a lode to mine, resting in the file cabinets and storage rooms of every FBO. What happened to all those former customers who never finished? Every one of those old logbooks and flight records represents someone who was once sold on flying, who budgeted time and money and committed to your training operation.

How many are lost forever? And how many would come back today, given the opportunity? Perhaps the biggest pool of qualified prospects in addition to your current students, are your former ones. Go through the records and call all of those inactive flight students.

The next, and perhaps most important message of this book, is that while bringing new customers out to the airport is critical for business growth, keeping our current students happy is imperative. It's a whole lot less expensive to solicit new business from current customers than to find new ones. And word-of-mouth sales come only through satisfied customers.

When students' flight training experiences are good, they complete their courses of training, come back to earn additional ratings, invest in aircraft rental and flight currency, purchase equipment and supplies, and perhaps ultimately buy aircraft.

Think of the economic return, if every student who began primary training actually finished the private pilot certificate, then went on to complete an instrument rating. Obviously we can't hope to keep everybody, but it's sure worth the "old college try" to retain more of them!

Why Students Quit

There are many reasons why people drop out of the training process. Some problems, like those involving money, health, or family, are obviously insurmountable for instructor or flight school to solve. The majority of flight students, however, quit for other reasons. "Quit" may actually be too strong a word, because so many of these people don't actually make a decision to stop flying. Rather, they just let the flying lapse, and never get back to it.

Why *do* so many students quit?

As host of a forum for new pilots on the biggest online service, I hear from many, many student pilots each month about why they have "put their flying on hold," or are thinking of quitting. It has been very enlightening for me to learn that the most common causes for students to quit flying are not necessarily what most of us expect. Let's take a look at the most common complaints I hear, and then consider what they mean:

"I was unhappy with my CFI, so I quit."

While it's not surprising that a certain percentage of students are dissatisfied with their instructors, what is unexpected is how they deal with it when it happens—they just quit! The obvious question for us to ponder is, why don't these students just switch to another instructor? And why don't they talk to anyone at the flight school before they quit?

"I've logged twenty hours of instruction, but still haven't soloed. My instructor says I'm doing fine, but my uncle who flew in WWII says eight hours is normal for solo."

Interestingly enough, while several students voicing such concerns have mentioned their large investment in flying to date, not one of them has complained about the cost. Rather, the issue seems to be, first, "Is there some reason why I may not be capable of being a pilot?" and then, "Am I getting ripped off?"

"How long should this be taking me?"

This is the single most common expression of concern I hear. Closely tied to the previous question, it again raises the issue of, "Am I on a par with everyone else?" Along with that concern is a major frustration, "I can't finish this darned thing!" A related concern I very often hear has to do with the knowledge test. Many students are extremely confused about the "best way" to study for the written, and as a result, find the practical test delayed for long periods of time as they grind to a halt while waffling over the knowledge test.

"My CFI left so I quit."

Again, these students very often don't seek out another instructor, nor do they tell anyone that they're quitting. Why not?

"After three CFIs in a row I left; the last one canceled every other lesson to go fly charters."

A variation on the last question, obviously tied to today's massive employee turnover among instructors. Translation: "No one cares about me or my flying."

Diverse as these questions may appear at first reading, there are actually some strong common threads between them. It doesn't take much reading between the lines to see that the concerns in every one of these cases boil down to just a few basic issues:

1. Students are not being adequately informed of their progress, including where they fall in the training process and clear identification of objectives yet to be accomplished.

2. Students feel they're being forced to depend solely upon the judgments of their instructors, with no validation from others.

3. There is no support structure within many students' flight schools to provide help and encouragement when they need it.

I'm sure everyone reading this can guess why some students might be taking so long to solo—maybe it's not flying often enough, or there was a break in training due to bad weather. Maybe there were learning plateaus which now have been surmounted, and some of these students are probably learning to fly in environments of complex airspace or high traffic density.

In short, any one of us could probably provide excellent encouragement to most students who think they're taking too long to solo—just by talking to them! Clearly, those who ask, "how long should this be taking?" are not being informed of their progress, including most specifically, what objectives must be accomplished in order for them to complete their training and earn their pilot certificates.

Maybe something else happened behind the scenes; perhaps there was a "bad lesson" which left the student questioning his or her abilities. Or perhaps a misunderstanding about a bill. But these reasons are surmountable too, given a courteous and understanding call from instructor or flight school.

Obviously the individual instructors are not doing the job right in most of these cases. But what each of us should be asking ourselves when we read these questions and comments is, "Where the heck is the flight school manager?!" And, "How many of these problems could he or she have easily solved, having known about them?"

USE PROACTIVE MANAGEMENT TO RETAIN CURRENT CUSTOMERS

Back in Chapter 8 we introduced the principle of proactive flight instructing: having every CFI act as mentor, cheerleader, counselor, consultant and advisor to students. Flight training managers can play an integral role in supporting this approach by training and inspiring their instructors and office staff, and through development of a structured customer retention policy.

Something's Missing From Your Training Syllabus!
Consider this scenario: a $4,000 customer walks into a business. The manager immediately turns the new customer over to a newly-graduated part-

time employee...never to follow up with the customer again! Sound familiar? It should, because this is exactly what happens all the time at many
flight schools.

When new students sign up for flying lessons they're assigned to individual CFIs and disappear into the maze of instructor cubicles, never to be
seen again. Everybody in management assumes that things are fine for the
duration of the student's training, unless or until some months down the
road, the student's name does come up again.

"Say, what ever happened to that Bill guy. Wasn't he flying with Jill?"

"You mean Bill, the tall guy? I don't know if anyone ever took him over
after Jill left."

Where did that customer go? Has he quit? If so, why? And how will the
flight school ever get him back as a customer?

Abandoning your customers solely to your instructors is extremely bad
policy. At issue is not whether individual CFIs can be entrusted to manage
their students, but rather the missed opportunities when no one else in the
flight school is communicating with that customer.

Therefore one major objective of every flight training manager should
be to develop a relationship with each training customer, *in addition* to the
student's association with his or her instructor.

The best way to accomplish this is for managers to schedule regular "customer satisfaction meetings" with each flight student as "part of the syllabus." These don't need to be part of your school's FAA-approved syllabus
paperwork, but they should be formalized in company policy:

"The flight training manager shall conduct a customer satisfaction meeting with each student immediately following every stage check. It will be
the instructor's responsibility to schedule these meetings."

Formalizing such sessions in the training program is important not only
to make sure they indeed happen, but also to ensure that everyone knows
about them in advance, including manager, student and instructor. When
everyone knows it's part of the routine, there's far less likelihood of inad-
vertently surprising or insulting anyone.

The stated purpose of these customer-manager meetings should simply be to ensure customer satisfaction, which in our business translates to student retention.

First, it's a sign of good service when company management periodically meets with its customers for purposes of quality control. Even when all's going well, a "How're things going?" meeting with the flight training manager tells each customer that "we care," also opening channels of communication should a problem occur later.

If the student *is* having a problem, the manager will hopefully learn of it during the meeting, so it can be addressed before the student gets aggravated and quits. The objective should be to draw student concerns of all kinds out into the open, so that there's an opportunity to solve them. We're not only talking flight training issues here, but also customer service problems, concerns about billing and accounts, maintenance issues, even crises of confidence in one's flying. If you as a manager just know in advance what a given student's problem is, there's a very good chance it can be solved and you keep that student's business.

Another important function of these periodic meetings is to back up the position of the CFI, thereby increasing the confidence of the student. "I've had twelve hours of flight instruction, and my instructor says it may be fifteen before I solo. But my uncle says he soloed in eight hours. Should I be concerned?" All too often the student has only the words of the instructor to act upon; sometimes a confirming, "second" opinion makes all the difference in the world when the customer has developed doubts.

And what if an instructor departs for greener pastures? Does anyone else at the flight school have a relationship established with her or his students? Not yet having much aviation experience, the average private pilot student tends to feel that her instructor is uniquely qualified to deal with her special situation and needs. As a result, when an instructor leaves, the students often founder. (This is especially true when an unfortunate student loses several instructors in a row.)

In these cases a friendly management contact in the flight school can save the day. The student has hopefully had at least a few meaningful conversations with someone who knows her situation, and who can recommend that "perfect" next instructor to keep things rolling along.

An additional benefit of regular student meetings is learning what your flight school is doing well. Knowing what makes your customers happy helps you hone your customer service and promotional programs. And if things are going well, what better time is there to ask your customers to refer their friends?

Ongoing CFI Training Program

Given the tremendous turnover among today's flight training employees, every flight school that wants to sustain its current customer base, simply must establish an ongoing continuing education program for its CFIs. Among the key objectives should be to train instructors to excel at customer service, and to thoroughly and consistently inform students of their progress.

An atmosphere of professionalism must be created among the CFI staff, which encourages open discussion of student problems, ease of transferring students between CFIs, when necessary, and smooth student hand-offs from departing instructors to someone the student is comfortable with.

Every pilot is accustomed to the concept of ongoing recurrent training, but generally it's considered solely in the context of flight skills. But with today's flight instructor turnover being what it is, we face a new challenge. Instructors hired today may work at the flight school for only a few months before moving on.

Never has there been a time when ongoing CFI training was more important. Flight students, particularly the mature ones who have the resources to become long-term customers, are more frustrated than ever about the difficulty of continuing their flight training in a progressive and uninterrupted manner.

Just as with line personnel and other high turnover employees, it's imperative that every flight training manager map out and establish a formal continuing education program for the CFI staff.

Schedule new employee training sessions on a regular basis, and formally program a weekly CFI "continuing education" program, built around the weekly staff flight instructor meeting.

Make That Weekly CFI Meeting a "Don't Miss It!" Event

Continuing education means, in the broadest sense, exposing your employees to new ideas every week, and reinforcing the best of the old ones. That means training in just about everything—student recruiting techniques, sales, customer service, professionalism, and of course, flight training methods.

The flight school benefits by increased new business and better customer retention. Students benefit through increased satisfaction and success in the flight training process, and instructors benefit from gaining knowledge and flight experience which will serve them through their careers.

CFI meeting topics can include any number of valuable and motivational subjects and speakers. Along with flight training topics such as methods for teaching specific maneuvers, CFI meetings should include designated examiners speaking on checkrides, aviation medical examiners (AMEs) speaking on medical requirements for certifying prospective students, CFI "training problems of the week," customer service and sales topics, and motivational speakers.

Where should the non-flying-topic speakers come from? Take advantage of the expertise of your customers! Among the students at most flight schools are successful business people who have caught the flying bug. Many have terrific experience in sales, customer relations, and other relevant topics. Invite them in, one at a time, to speak at your CFI meetings. Learn about how different business people sell their products and services, and how they satisfy their customers.

Stage Checks are Mandatory

For the reasons we have discussed, stage checks are imperative for all flight training. Whether or not yours is an "FAA-approved" flight program, someone sharp needs to professionally interact with each student, both on the ground and in the air, several times during training.

It is absolutely imperative that your stage check system *validates CFI opinions and performance for each student*. That means involving students in their phase check debriefings, so customers can see that their personal training status and objectives are agreed upon by both personal flight instructor and stage check instructor. The CFI, customer, and flight training manager must all know where each student is in the training process, all of the time.

Every Flight School Needs a Ground School Policy

It is very important for purposes of student retention to formally integrate ground school into every flight school's training programs. The type of ground school, be it organized classroom, integrated multimedia, or even home study, is not as important as the fact that such a program exists. Every flight training customer must know from day one exactly how he or she will complete training for both the knowledge test, and the oral portion of the practical test.

One Flight School's Innovative Instruction Rules

For purposes of bringing all this together, let's take a look at one flight school's instruction policies, which codify many of the proactive management issues we've just addressed into a comprehensive program.

Many pilot training programs incorporate some of the individual rules described here, but what makes this school innovative is the comprehensive structure of policies designed to keep customers satisfied, optimize their training, and motivate staff CFIs, all while enhancing profitability.

The following policies are courtesy of Flightstar, Champaign, Illinois. They are presented in letter form, as I received them, so as to retain the illuminating comments of Warren Smith, the school's flight training manager.

Greg,

We have tried many different approaches to common flight training problems. Here are some that actually work. By the way, the list of ideas that did not work is much larger.

<u>Instructor Time Cards</u>: Instructors fill out time cards for each lesson. The cards show the lesson starting time, ending time, and aircraft Hobbs time. At the end of the lesson the cards are given to the receptionist. The receptionist subtracts the total lesson time from the aircraft Hobbs time to get the ground instruction time and charges the student accordingly. For example: a lesson starts at 8:00 and ends at 10:00 and includes a one hour flight. The receptionist would charge the student for one hour of aircraft rental and two hours of instruction. The bottom line here is that the student is charged for the entire time that they are with the instructor.

One important aspect of this process is that all students are told up front that if they feel that they are being improperly charged or have any complaints that they can come and talk to me. I also check in with students periodically with a phone call to ensure that they are satisfied with their training.

The time cards have had several positive effects on our flight training department:

• Our instruction billings have tripled.

• Instructors are forced to be prepared for lessons; if they are not, and the student is charged, I am going to hear about it.

• Instructors can no longer sit inside and sip coffee while their students are out preflighting. Since we are charging for this time, the instructor is required to be with the student. The instructors take advantage of this time to quiz their students and answer questions.

• Instructors must start and stop lessons on schedule.

• Instructors make more money, Flightstar makes more money.

- They remove the pressure from the instructor of having to decide what amount of time should be billed. I have found that many instructors feel guilty about charging customers.
- Because students are going to be charged, they are more likely to show up for a lesson prepared. In fact, we always tell students that the best way to save money is to do the homework.

The best part about this whole thing is that I have yet to have any complaints!

Instant Gratification: This day and age people want instant results. They buy a $6,000 dollar jet ski and they are instantly at the lake having fun. They could easily learn to fly for the same amount of money, but it might take them six months to a year to get the license. That's an eternity by today's standards. At Flightstar we work very hard at incorporating instant gratification into our flight training. We have broken our Private Pilot's license down into five "Flightsteps." When a student completes a Flightstep we make a huge deal out of it and let them know that they have really accomplished something.

Student No-Shows: We tell the students (and give them a policy paper) that if they fail to give us at least twelve hours notice of cancellation that, at the instructors discretion, they may be charged up to one hour of ground instruction. We try to be pretty lenient with this but if a student blatantly blows us off, or repeatedly misses lessons, we charge them.

Money on Account: We don't do it anymore. First, all students and renter pilots are required to keep a credit card on file with us. Then, a student can either pay as they go or have the charges billed to their credit card after each lesson. A student has two options: pay as you fly, or keep a credit card on file with us so each flight can be billed to the credit card. Ninety percent of our students have their charges billed directly to the credit cards. Eliminating student accounts has eliminated bad debt completely.

90 Day Checkout Requirement: All renter pilots must have flown our airplane within the last ninety days to continue renting. If not, then they must complete another checkout. In addition they must be current in each type of aircraft they want to rent. If they are current in the Archer, they cannot necessarily go fly the Warrior; they must also be 90 day current in the Warrior. In addition, all renter pilots must have a credit card on file with us.

90 Day Probation: All of our instructors go through a 90-day probationary period. At the end of the 90 days we give them a thorough performance review. If they don't measure up we send them on their way.

Instructors Only Instruct: We do not require our instructors to do any selling, maintenance, scheduling, line service work, or any other duties other than instructing. Their mission is simple: provide safe, effective training using Flightstar's standardized format.

Instructor Meetings: Every Monday morning at 8:00 a.m. we have a one hour instructors meeting. We review each student and discuss their progress as well as review the week's schedule. We also discuss any problems that may be occurring and the maintenance status of each aircraft. The meetings follow a standardized format so that if I am unable to attend a senior instructor can conduct the meeting and report back to me. Immediately following every instructor meeting I have a short meeting with the maintenance department to coordinate any inspections or unscheduled maintenance.

Zero Tolerance Maintenance: We do not tolerate anything broken on an airplane. If a sticker is missing or worn we replace it. Instructors tend to ignore minor maintenance problems for some reason. We have to constantly remind them to write things up.

Dress Code: We require instructors to wear dress shoes, dress pants, long sleeve shirt and a tie. In the summer months they have the option of wearing a Flightstar logo polo shirt (that we sell to them at cost), walking shoes, and "docker"-type pants.

Sales Tracking: We use ACT! to track all of our sales leads. Any-one who contacts us is kept in the database and followed up on as required.

Instructor Pay: We have established a minimum monthly revenue target that we expect each instructor to meet. Instructors are paid a base salary plus additional hourly amounts for exceeding the mini-mum revenue hours.

Goal Setting: All instructors are required to set goals with their students. These goals might include when a student will solo or when they will get their license. Progress toward these goals is discussed during the instructor meetings. When someone does not meet a goal we investigate why and try to make improvements so it does not happen again.

Instructor Turnover: We just accept it as part of the business. We are constantly looking for new instructors. If we run across some-one that really impresses us, we hire them whether we need them or not; eventually we are going to need them and good flight in-structors are hard to find.

Instructor Burn-out: Our instructors are assigned one day off per week and rotate weekends off. When instructors work seven days a week their activity levels spike up and down.

Some people will go somewhere else because of our prices. Some people may be turned off by some of our policies. But that's O.K. It took me a long time to accept that.

Warren

KEEP THOSE CUSTOMERS FLYING

Host Social Events

How many times have you seen two pilots meet — and then have nothing to talk about? I'm sure you'll agree that's a rare occurrence. It's to the benefit of every flight training business for its pilot customers to meet one another.

At least one flight school I know of hosts a social gathering for its flight students every month. This is a terrific idea because giving students an opportunity to meet each other creates an instant support network for sharing of concerns and encouragement.

New prospective pilots get the opportunity to meet current students, and learn what it's all about. Remember, the most enthusiastic pilots out there are those with fresh solo endorsements and temporary airman certificates in their wallets. Let them do some selling!

Current pilots benefit by meeting their peers, too. It's an opportunity to line up new friends to fly with, safety pilots, and expense-sharing partners.

Another benefit of this gathering is that it offers yet one more opportunity for the flight school staff to get to know individual customers. We discussed earlier the importance of developing relationships between students and flight school managers, as well as with other CFIs in addition to their own.

Among other flight school social opportunities are gatherings for special purposes, like hosting a customer focus group session for the purpose of improving customer service. Then there are educational gatherings, such as a "meet the examiner" coffee so students can get comfortable with the person who will be conducting their checkrides. Meetings with designated medical examiners draw plenty of interest, too.

Make Rental Planes Available

We talked earlier about the condition of a flight school's aircraft relative to selling new training customers on flying lessons. A related subject is the need to have a nice fleet of rental aircraft available for pilots to use after earning their ratings.

Five or ten years ago a pilot could go to most FBOs and find any number of rental aircraft to choose from, ranging from two-seaters to light twins. But those days are largely gone. Between the diminishing number of available clean aircraft, increasing insurance premiums, and obstructive rental policies, it is increasingly difficult to rent a plane with adequate performance and availability for pilots to travel anywhere.

This problem is of rapidly-growing concern among pilots who aren't in a position to own their own aircraft. If you can't access a plane to go anywhere, why be a pilot? Without a rental fleet, there are no students for advanced ratings, no customers for aviation supplies and equipment, and no future airplane buyers.

Flight schools wanting to keep their general aviation clientele flying simply must have a rental fleet—not just trainers, but aircraft of adequate quality and capability so customers will feel comfortable inviting their families and business associates to travel with them.

Retain Customers Through Fun and Adventure

Growing numbers of flight schools are organizing flying adventures for their customers, most built around travel by plane to interesting destinations. By planning such trips, negotiating group rates, and making all the reservations, many FBOs have had good success in getting their customers to rent a group of airplanes and fly somewhere. We in the business can do a lot more in this regard, by organizing other interesting flying activities like rallies and races, and competitions like precision landings and flour-sack bombing.

One flight school I know of is in the process of putting together a brilliantly clever flight incentive booklet for new private pilots graduating from their program. Modeled after those "dining club" coupon books many of us buy (you know, the kind filled with "buy one meal, get the second one free" tickets), the new booklet includes coupons the flight school has negotiated at interesting cross-country destinations within several hundred miles of their airport.

Along with discounts at restaurants, museums, parks and tourist attractions, the booklet includes miscellaneous planning tidbits for each trip, such as magnetic course from the home airport, and good places to stay once you get there.

But here's the best part. Not only do the newly-certificated pilots get discounts for visiting all sorts of interesting destinations, but upon completing all flights in the book, they have accumulated the cross-country pilot-in-command flight experience required to qualify for the instrument rating. Can you beat that? Not only does this program rent planes for the FBO, but it increases the attraction of training for the next rating, all the while delivering real flying enjoyment to pilots and their friends and families.

THIRTEEN

Business and Professional Opportunities: Your Future as an Instructor

In recent years the phrases, "flight training," "business opportunities," and "professional careers," were rarely heard together in the same conversation. But that situation is rapidly changing.

Flight training is on a roll that promises to continue well into the future, and with it comes opportunity at two levels—the chance for flight schools to grow through a greatly broadened customer base, and new promise for pilots interested in pursuing professional instructing careers.

Opportunity is a hard thing to predict, and you can bet that many in the industry are warming up their thinking caps as you read this, with an eye toward tapping all that new business potential. In this chapter we'll just skim the surface as to what some of those new business and professional opportunities in flight training may be.

FLIGHT TRAINING BUSINESS OPPORTUNITIES

With the resumption of large-scale light aircraft manufacturing and the advent of new industry programs for recruiting students, the flight training industry faces new opportunities for growth. As host of a nationwide online learn-to-fly forum, I've learned a good deal about potential market opportunities, some of which are fairly obvious, and others surprising. The most exciting news is that there are still many, many people itching to fly. But the challenge for many flight schools will be to engage gears with open minds and perhaps new attitudes about our customers. Here are several groups which promise to bring new business to aviation.

Women and Minorities

Among the most enthusiastic of today's pilots are women. Finally it has become acceptable for women to become pilots, and as more and more of them enter the pilot ranks, their less adventurous peers have become more interested in pursuing flight, too. But many of the female flight training customers out there are very unhappy with their treatment at various flight schools. As car dealers learned about ten years ago, women must be made to feel welcome and comfortable in businesses that hope to earn their dollars. And few flight schools have made specific efforts to understand, identify, and attract female and minority customers.

At the most basic level, it is becoming more and more important, from a marketing standpoint, that flight schools have some female pilots on staff. It should be obvious that women who may be hesitant to learn to fly, are encouraged when they meet others like themselves who are not only pilots, but have reached professional status as instructors.

Other aspects to such issues may be less obvious. I recently heard from a highly enthusiastic female student pilot who wanted to travel to the sunny locale where I fly, to complete her private pilot training. Her hometown weather had been terrible over the preceding few months, and she'd become frustrated by the resulting training delays. After a good deal of discussion about possible instructors in my geographic area, she mentioned her interest in meeting some local members of the "Ninety-Nines" women pilots association. When I mentioned the names of a few Ninety-Nines who are CFIs, she responded enthusiastically.

Only then did it come out that the student's husband was uncomfortable with the idea of his wife spending many hours in close contact with a male flight instructor. (And what's a training aircraft, if not close quarters?) While this is hopefully an isolated case, the fact remains that different students have different concerns, and that the more diverse a flight school staff, the broader its clientele is likely to be also.

Do you have any Spanish-speaking instructors on staff? Any African-Americans? This is a great way to bring more minorities to general aviation.

Young Pilot "Wannabes"

> "OK, here's the deal … i'm 13 years old, and i live for airplanes. I've flown them before, but now i want my own plane … I've been trying to convince my parents to get me an ultralight for my Bar-Mitzvah present, but it hasn't been going to good … If you could come up with a stratigy, or some good points about an ultralight … it would be most apprieciated. Their just soo nervous about me being in a plane by my self … with out a liscence. Thanks for reading my mail …
> ~bye for now~ … David Goodman"

Every red-blooded flight instructor knows exactly how young David Goodman felt when he wrote that letter, but few of us adults could express it nearly as well.

It's probably no surprise to anyone that kids are interested in flying, but not everyone realizes just how many high school and junior high students want to become pilots, and how fanatically committed they are to doing it. Not only have many of these kids mastered every flight simulation computer program known to cyberspace, but they hang around the aviation online chat rooms, conversing with real pilots about the details of every sort of aircraft from Cherokees to Boeings, and F-16s to Apache helicopters.

These young enthusiasts own large collections of videotapes and books. They con their parents into attending every airshow within hundreds of miles, can argue the finer points of stealth technology on the F-22 fighter, and spend hours every day monitoring the local control tower frequency — when not watching aviation programs on the Discovery Channel, that is.

Many young people have already determined the sort of professional flying they want to do; in fact a surprising number have already selected the specific airline they plan to fly for one day, or are already hard at work building qualifications for the Air Force or Naval Academies.

The bad news is that few of the kids I hear from feed their aviation habits at the local airport. With the exception of a few youth-oriented programs like EAA's Young Eagles program and Civil Air Patrol's cadet squadrons, most kids have nowhere to go to get involved in aviation.

While a few flight schools do address young pilots — one in my own community has set up a joint program with an aviation magnet school, and goes so far as to provide after-school transportation to the airport — this is the exception, not the rule. Most flight schools and instructors appear to be letting a very large market slip away in their local communities. That's bad for business, bad for young "wannabe" pilots and bad for the future of general aviation.

How can instructors capitalize on the opportunity? The answer is simple. Every flight school should be offering organized and regularly-scheduled aviation youth activities at the airport, with the objective to get those young pilot hopefuls (and their parents, whenever possible) directly and regularly involved in aviation. This can be done through tie-in with local magnet school programs and after-school aviation clubs. Or your flight school can sponsor an Aviation Explorers Post, a Civil Air Patrol Cadet Squadron, or some sort of independent "young aviators" club.

"What's in it for me?" instructors might legitimately ask. Along with the altruistic but important mission of building aviation for the future, there are quite a few practical reasons for developing youth-based aviation programs.

The most immediate conventional return from an active youth aviation club comes in the form of intro lessons. Teens join such an organization because they want to fly, so organizing activities for them indeed gets instructors and airplanes up into the air.

Once the program gets rolling, you'll also gain opportunities to sign up family and friends for flying lessons. Somebody's been driving those kids to the airshows, buying them flight simulator games, and generally sharing the dream of flight. Those folks are prospects, too. (Consider offering a "learn to fly together" deal for students and their parents.)

Perhaps most astonishing is the number of teenagers who are taking flying lessons, even when several years away from being old enough to qualify for airplane category pilot certificates.

High school students can afford to take flying lessons? Any doubters should run down to the local high school and check out the vehicles cruising through the parking lot. At a time when a cheap used car costs more than private pilot training, plenty of students can come up with the money to fly, either by working or with help from Mom and Dad.

Part of the trick, of course, is for parents to understand the benefits of having their sons and daughters take flying lessons while still in high school. Here's the pitch to help kids in your new aviation youth program sell their folks on training.

First, point out that becoming a pilot is a challenging and worthwhile learning experience which ties in wonderfully with academic subjects like math and science, and also builds important personal skills such as decision-making and the setting and achievement of goals.

For students interested in pursuing a flying career, there are additional benefits to earning their private certificates while still in high school, such as helping them get accepted to a university flight program or military academy. Getting into the better programs can be tough, and students already holding a pilot certificate at time of application have an edge over the competition.

It's also worth pointing out that university flight programs generally issue college credit for completed pilot ratings held by incoming students.

Since earning a private certificate at the local FBO usually costs less than doing it at college, students can often save money by training while still in high school. Certificated pilots entering college also find themselves ahead of their aviation classmates in that they can start instructing earlier in their college careers, thereby building experience and earning income sooner.

Aviation club students who are not yet ready to start lessons offer business opportunities of their own. Who says that instructors and flight schools must make their money only through flying? It's perfectly appropriate to charge reasonable fees for classes, field trips, and other activities, plus selling aviation T-shirts, software, and goodies at the pilot shop. And don't forget ground schools. Since the knowledge test results are good for two years, it's feasible to offer private pilot classes to older teens.

Finally, your youth club members are tomorrow's flight training customers. Along with the young people who begin taking lessons almost immediately upon joining the club, quite a few more will be ready to invest in flight training within only a year or two. Many of us in aviation are notoriously shortsighted—if it's not about today's flight or tomorrow's lesson, it's just not important.

But youth programs offer the opportunity to groom today's aviation enthusiasts into tomorrow's customers. Anyone with even the slightest knack for business should appreciate what an important opportunity that is. It's in everyone's interest to begin selling a new generation of pilots—and their parents—on flying.

Quick Completion Training Programs

One other perhaps neglected training opportunity area addresses one of the bigger complaints of student training, "I can't finish this darned pilot training!" Students are not completing their certificates nearly as soon as they would like to.

As we've discussed several times in the course of this book, people enroll for flying lessons to become pilots, not students, so the longer it takes to train them through to their target certificates, the greater the likelihood of losing them.

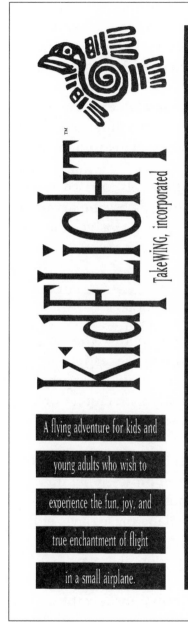

Give the gift they will never forget!

Your KidFLIGHT™package includes:

(Tailored to the age and experience level of the flyer)

✈ A preflight inspection of the airplane along with an explanation of the flight instruments and a fun introduction to aerodynamics.

✈ A special headset to communicate in the plane and listen to air traffic control throughout the flight.

✈ A guided hands-on lesson on how to taxi the airplane.

✈ An exciting aerial tour where they will find a favorite landmark (school, house, park, etc.), and under supervision of the pilot, feel what it's like to actually fly the airplane. Plus, as they return to Creswell you'll hear them as they broadcast their landing to the air traffic control area over our office speakers!

✈ A sparkling cider reception, a TakeWING certificate of accomplishment, and two Polaroid photos: One in the pilot's seat, and one in front of the airplane upon landing—thumbs up, of course!

Each flight is tailored to the age and experience level of our passenger so he or she will get the most from this experience. Though a parent or guardian is welcome to ride-a-long for no additional charge, we have found that much of the thrill this adventure has to offer lies in the young aviator experiencing it by themselves, and sharing it with you later.

Your KidFLIGHT™ flying adventure is only $85

Attractive gift certificates and group discounts are available.

TakeWING, Inc. brings the dream and enchantment of flight to you through customized flight training experiences. All flights depart from the Creswell Airport, only 10 minutes from Eugene. In the event of bad weather or other adverse conditions we have the right to delayed or rescheduled flights. A liability waiver is required prior to participation. For reservations or further information about KidFLIGHT™, WomanFLIGHT™, ClassicFLIGHT™, AbleFLIGHT™, or our other flight training adventures, please give us a call.

Call us at 555-9464

Dorothy Schick, President of TakeWING, Inc. is a licensed commercial pilot and certificated flight instructor. She is an active member of the 99's, Airplane Owners and Pilots Association, and the Experimental Aircraft Association. She has been living and flying in the area for over 20 years.

TakeWING, Inc. "Adventure Flight" targeting young people. Those completing the flight are issued a "KidFlight Pilot's License," to carry in their wallets. The flight school also offers a number of aviation camps for young people. (For other TakeWING Adventure Flights, see Chapter 5.)

Private pilots, in particular, often suffer tremendous difficulties in completing their certificates, especially in parts of the country and at times of year when weather is bad. One Minnesota flight school manager told me recently that losing customers in the winter is just part of doing business in the North.

As a result of these sorts of problems, there seems to be a strong, and perhaps growing opportunity for more schools to offer intensive quick completion training courses, especially at the private and instrument training levels.

Aside from the obvious opportunity for flight schools in fair-weather locations to promote winter-time short courses, there may be similar opportunities for those in colder climates to offer a series of intensive summertime courses. "Make hay while the sun shines," one might say.

NEW OPPORTUNITIES: PILOT TRAINING CAREERS

Strange as it may sound to some, there are actually pilots who love instructing enough to make a career out of it. And if you're one of those people who enjoy teaching in aviation, the market for your services is growing daily. Training is probably the hottest growth industry in aviation. Aircraft are becoming ever more sophisticated, requiring more and more extensive pilot training.

Where pilots could make do with a simple instructor checkout in the old days, the insurance industry now requires extensive professional training before they'll cover sophisticated private and corporate aircraft.

Pilot education isn't limited to just flying the plane these days, either. Special training is required for today's glass cockpits and flight management systems. Then there's the continually-growing emphasis on "CRM" training, crew resource management for multi-pilot crews. The latest development is aircraft-upset training: how to recover from unusual attitudes in transport category aircraft. As the number and depth of pilot qualifications continue to increase, the rate of demand for training professionals is going through the roof.

Then there's the FAA's recent "one level of safety" initiative, a rewrite of the regulations which requires that operators of smaller commuter airline aircraft meet the same extensive training standards as major airline operators.

With all this happening, plus the current aviation boom, the demand for professional instructors is growing like never before, with the result that pay and benefits for professional positions are rapidly improving.

Airline Training Departments

Have you ever thought about who does the training at the airlines? Sure, experienced line pilots serve as check airmen in the aircraft, but who teaches at the training center?

Those people come from a variety of backgrounds, but a surprising number are flight instructors like you and I, who have been hired directly into airline training departments. If you have several years and several thousand hours of flight instructing experience, and have done some classroom teaching along the way, the airlines might very well be a teaching option to investigate.

Benefits of such positions usually include flight and jumpseating privileges on the airline, discount travel on other airlines, and sometimes, potential to ultimately transfer from the training department to a line pilot position with the airline.

Flight Training Managers

Then there are the all the flight schools. We seem to be in a period of consolidation, with many formerly small FBOs gearing up larger programs for training of more students. At the same time, the large flight schools are growing even bigger. Someone has to manage each of those programs. Not only does the FAA require a Chief Flight Instructor to meet certain experience qualifications for every "approved" flight school, but even those not seeking approved status require quality training people to manage their growing programs.

Simulator and Pilot Proficiency Companies

The days of pilots spending many hours flight-training in sophisticated aircraft are long gone. Nowadays virtually all training for advanced aircraft is done in flight simulators, and the proliferation of companies in this business has been nothing short of amazing.

Not only is most FAA-required airline and corporate flight training now done in simulators, but insurance company-mandated requirements are growing rapidly at the same time.

As a result, the aviation magazines are filled with ads for simulator instructors. Many of these positions pay extremely well, and have excellent benefits.

International Opportunities

Impressive as aviation growth in our own country has been, it pales by comparison with other places in the world. Growth of commercial aviation in the Far East, for example, is expected to outstrip all other parts of the globe for many years to come.

But most of the countries where growth is expected to be greatest have virtually no indigenous pilot population, nor programs for training them. As a result, contract pilot training for foreign countries and carriers, performed both here and abroad, offers tremendous growth and career potential for those who are interested.

FOURTEEN

Legacy of an Instructor: the Privilege and the Glory

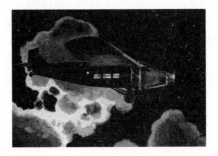

Every now and then one meets a young commercial pilot who trumpets to anyone who will listen, "I'm looking for a way to skip flight instructing and get on to the real flying."

Most people who feel that way are making a terrible mistake, because serving as a CFI is one of the great experiences of a pilot career. It really is true that the best way to learn a subject is to teach it; your hours spent training others to fly will repay you many times over in knowledge, judgment and lessons learned.

Along with sharpening a pilot's technical knowledge, flight instructing teaches the human element of flying in a way that nothing else can. With it comes understanding of important principles of leadership, crew coordination, and flight safety. Flight instructing teaches the difficult balance of depending on others, how to give people the freedom and responsibility to act, while at the same time carefully monitoring their performance.

If you think no one else will ever care whether you flight instruct or not, you're wrong. CFI experience is considered a big plus for virtually any flight position you'll ever apply for. One reason is that at least some if not all pilot training at most flight departments is done in-house, so teaching experience is a valuable asset. Employers also anticipate deeper aeronautical knowledge from experienced instructors, and better communication skills.

Then there's the social element. The aviation community is a small one, so friends you make as you teach them to fly, and as they teach you, will reappear time and again throughout your flying career. Former students will help get you jobs, and you'll help them. Familiar faces will appear on airport ramps at exotic places, and in living color on the pages of industry magazines.

Several years ago, I opened *Flying*, *AOPA Pilot*, and *Air & Space*, all in the same month, only to discover one of my long-ago private pilot students smiling back at me, as a prominent member of the U.S. Aerobatic Team. I'd like to tell you that I taught her everything she knows, but it would be a lie. She took private pilot training from me, then moved on to bigger and better things. But I'm proud of being part of her aviation heritage, all the same.

The pride that comes with such a discovery is difficult to convey to new instructors, but when it happens to you a few years down the line, you'll feel sorry for anyone who hasn't personally experienced it. Nine times out of ten, when I hear what a former student is doing, it's pretty exciting stuff.

I gave one young student just two introductory flying lessons several years ago while he was in town for a visit, and in the process changed his life forever. He recently hired on with a major airline flying Boeing 737s, at the incredibly young age of twenty-six.

Then there's my former part-time flight instructor from college days, who is now a pilot for Continental Airlines. During a recent visit we reminisced about flying together years ago. When I complimented him on his accomplishment in making it to the majors, he said, "Hey, I'm there because of you!"

"How do you figure that?" I asked in astonishment.

He then reminded me of the time after college when I invited him to join me for a flight to Atlantic City in a Piper Navajo, the one time I gave him flight instruction, instead of the other way around. "That was my first multi-engine dual," he told me, "and on the basis of that flight I decided to become a professional pilot. Remember? A knob fell off the DME on our take-off from Columbus, Ohio."

Of course I didn't remember the knob falling off, nor even that we had made that flight together until my friend reminded me of the details. After all, it was a long time ago. But he's never forgotten.

All of this comes back to something we considered in the opening pages of this book. Remember that lesson you're giving tomorrow? For you, it may register only as another entry in your logbook. But it's entirely possible that the life of your student will change forever because of that flight. That he or she might find a new calling. Or perhaps save hundreds of people's lives because of something learned at that lesson with a savvy CFI.

Flight instructing is a heck of a responsibility, a heck of a privilege, and a heck of an opportunity. Make the most of it!

ABOUT THE AUTHOR

Greg Brown's love for flying is obvious in every section of this book, as is his concern for the image of the flight instructor and flight school: that they perform the best they can to seek out, promote, and sustain the joy of flight for the good of the entire industry.

In keeping with his role as general aviation advocate, Greg hosts the "Aviation Careers Forum" and the "New Pilots Forum" on America Online, and serves as a Contributing Editor for *Flight Training* magazine. He has entertained and educated aviation audiences as a speaker since 1990, most recently as presenter for NATA's acclaimed Flight School Manager Training Seminars.

An active practitioner of the noble art of flight instructing since 1979, Greg has also served as a professional pilot in both scheduled and corporate aviation, and flown extensively for pleasure and personal business. His teaching background also includes service as faculty member at Purdue University, regular presentations at Embry-Riddle Aeronautical University, and numerous professional seminars.

Greg Brown earned Bachelor's and Master's degrees at the University of Illinois at Urbana-Champaign, where his graduate work included human-factors cockpit design at the Aviation Research Laboratory. He also studied for two years at the University of Wisconsin-Madison, and completed several advanced flight ratings at Purdue University. He holds an ATP pilot certificate with Boeing 737 type rating, and a Flight Instructor certificate with all fixed wing aircraft ratings including glider. Greg also holds Advanced and Instrument Ground Instructor ratings, and has been active as a pilot since 1971.

Other popular aviation books by Gregory N. Brown include *The Turbine Pilot's Flight Manual*, and *Job Hunting for Pilots*.